RONALD

REAGAN

RONALD REAGAN

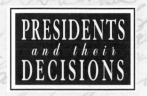

PRESIDENTS
and their
DECISIONS

RONALD
REAGAN

JAMES D. TORR, *Book Editor*

DAVID L. BENDER, *Publisher*
BRUNO LEONE, *Executive Editor*
BONNIE SZUMSKI, *Editorial Director*
STUART B. MILLER, *Managing Editor*

GREENHAVEN PRESS, INC.
SAN DIEGO, CALIFORNIA

Every effort has been made to trace the owners of copyrighted material. The articles in this volume may have been edited for content, length, and/or reading level. The titles have been changed to enhance the editorial purpose.

Library of Congress Cataloging-in-Publication Data

Ronald Reagan / James D. Torr, book editor.
    p.   cm. — (Presidents and their decisions)
    Includes bibliographical references and index.
    ISBN 0-7377-0501-9 (pbk. : alk. paper) — ISBN 0-7377-0502-7
(lib. : alk. paper)
    1. Reagan, Ronald. 2. United States—Politics and government—
1981–1989—Decision making. I. Torr, James D., 1974– . II. Series.

E876 .R645 2001
973.927'092—dc21

99-086357
CIP

Cover photo: C. Wally McNamee/CORBIS
Ronald Reagan Library 17, 23, 31, 194, 203, 213
Terry Arthur/White House 93

Series Design: LiMiTeD Edition Book Design, Linda Mae Tratechaud

©2001 Greenhaven Press, Inc.
P.O. Box 289009, San Diego, CA 92198-9009

PRINTED IN THE U.S.A.

Contents

Chapter 1: Reaganomics

In his first inaugural speech Ronald Reagan proclaimed,
"Government is not the solution to our problem; government is the problem." The Reagan administration favored
reducing taxes and cutting unnecessary federal programs.
In advocating a turn away from government, Reagan
became the first president to openly oppose Franklin
Roosevelt's New Deal of the 1930s.

Reagan's economic policies were based on the theory of
supply-side economics, which holds that cutting taxes
can help boost the economy. Reagan's 1981 tax cut
helped initiate "the Reagan boom," the largest surge in
the U.S. economy since World War II.

Ronald Reagan came into office promising to cut taxes,
reduce government spending, increase defense spending,
and balance the budget. However, the promises of
supply-side economics proved hollow; under Reagan
taxes were cut while government spending increased, and
as a result the national debt soared.

The main legacy of Reaganomics is increased economic
inequality. Reagan's tax cuts favored the very rich more
than they did the middle class, and his efforts to eliminate "big government" harmed the poor, since they usu-

ally involved eliminating social programs such as welfare and school lunches.

CHAPTER 2: THE END OF THE COLD WAR

threat and, if anything, this reduced their willingness to discuss arms control.

CHAPTER 3: THE IRAN-CONTRA AFFAIR

CHAPTER 4: THE GREAT COMMUNICATOR

the same way that an actor relies on a script and a director. The president's acting skills also account for his success with the media, since a trained actor is always conscious of appearing his best.

FOREWORD

"THE PRESIDENCY OF THE UNITED STATES IS OFTEN DE-scribed as the most powerful office in the world," writes Forrest McDonald in *The American Presidency: An Intellectual History*. "In one sense this description is accurate," he says, "for even casual decisions made in the White House can affect the lives of millions of people." But McDonald also notes that presidential power "is restrained by the countervailing power of Congress, the courts, the bureaucracy, popular opinion, the news media, and state and local governments. What presidents do have is awesome responsibilities combined with unique opportunities to persuade others to do their bidding—opportunities enhanced by the possibility of dispensing favors, by the mystique of presidential power, and by the aura of monarchy that surrounds the president."

The way various presidents have used the complex power of their office is the subject of Greenhaven Press's Presidents and Their Decisions series. Each volume in the series examines one particular president and the key decisions he made while in office.

Some presidential decisions have been made in a relatively brief period of time, as with Abraham Lincoln's suspension of the writ of habeus corpus at the start of the Civil War. Others were refined as they were implemented over a period of years, as was the case with Franklin Delano Roosevelt's struggle to lead the country out of the Great Depression. Some presidential actions are generally lauded by historians—for example, Lyndon Johnson's support of the civil rights movement in the 1960s—while others have been condemned—such as Richard Nixon's efforts, from 1972 to 1974, to cover up the involvement of his aides in the Watergate scandal.

Most of the truly history-making presidential decisions, though, remain the subject of intense scrutiny and historical debate. Many of these were made during a time of war or other crisis, in which a president was forced to risk either spectacular success or devastating failure. Examples include Lincoln's much-scrutinized handling of the crisis at Fort Sumter, the first conflict of the Civil War; FDR's efforts to aid the European Allies at the beginning of World War II; Harry Truman's controversial decision to use the atomic bomb in order to end that conflict; and Lyndon Johnson's fateful decision to escalate the war in Vietnam.

Each volume in the Presidents and Their Decisions series devotes a full chapter to each of the president's key decisions. The essays in each chapter, most written by presidential historians and biographers, offer a range of perspectives on the president and his actions. Some provide background on the political, social, and economic factors behind a particular decision. Others critique the president's performance, offering a negative or positive appraisal. Essays have been chosen for their concise and engaging presentation of the facts, and each is preceded by a straightforward summary of the article's content.

In addition to the articles, these books include extensive material to help the student researcher. An opening essay provides both a brief biography of the president and an overview of the events that occurred during his time in office. A chronology also helps readers keep track of the dates of specific events. A comprehensive index and an annotated table of contents aid readers in quickly locating material of interest, and an extensive bibliography serves as a launching point for further research. Finally, an appendix of primary historical documents provides a sampling of the president's most important speeches, as well as some of his contemporaries' criticisms.

Greenhaven Press's Presidents and Their Decisions series will help students gain a deeper understanding of the decisions made by some of the most influential leaders in American history.

INTRODUCTION

R ONALD REAGAN WAS ONE OF THE MOST POPULAR PRESI-
dents in recent history. He was the first two-term
president since Dwight Eisenhower left office in 1961. Because of his economic policies and his inspirational
speeches, which focused on patriotism, the importance of
family and religion, and the need for limited government,
the "Reagan years" have come to symbolize a rebirth of the
Republican Party in American politics. And in his meetings
with Soviet leader Mikhail Gorbachev, Reagan presided
over one of the most dramatic shifts in international relations since World War II. His accomplishments, and the
controversies surrounding them, have made the Reagan
presidency a lively subject for historical debate.

Early Life

Ronald Wilson Reagan was born on February 6, 1911, and
grew up in the small town of Dixon, Illinois. His father,
Jack, was a shoe salesman and his mother, Nelle, was a fer-
vently religious member of the Disciples of Christ Church.
Many of Reagan's biographers have speculated on how the
future president's upbringing shaped his adult personality:
The consensus is that his mother imbued her son with religious faith and a strong sense of optimism, while his father the salesman taught Ronald the skills of showmanship
that would later serve him as an actor and as president.
Some have also speculated that Jack Reagan's alcoholism
had a profound effect on the future president. "He developed a protective barrier between himself and other
people," writes William E. Pemberton, author of *Exit with
Honor: The Life and Presidency of Ronald Reagan*, noting
that "children of alcoholics sometimes escape into 'little

worlds' of fantasy."[1] Friends and associates throughout his life noted that while Reagan was always amiable and outgoing, he formed few close relationships with anybody.

Ronald Reagan, along with his brother, Neil, attended Eureka College. After graduating in 1932, Reagan became a sports announcer for a small radio station in Davenport, Iowa, and soon was broadcasting on a larger station in Des Moines. While many Americans were struggling to get by during the Great Depression, Reagan was becoming a minor celebrity in the Midwest. His father, however, lost his position as a salesman in 1932. He struggled for a time, but was finally able to find work through one of President Franklin Delano Roosevelt's New Deal relief agencies. The episode led both Jack Reagan and his son Ronald to become lifelong admirers of Roosevelt.

Hollywood

In 1937, a friend introduced Ronald Reagan to a Hollywood agent who got him a screen test with Warner Brothers movie studio. The fortuitous meeting marked the beginning of Reagan's decade-long career in Hollywood. In total, he starred in fifty-three films. "On screen, he often portrayed characters who responded to danger or adversity with a wisecrack followed by a 'pep talk,'" writes Michael Schaller in his book *Reckoning with Reagan*, "gradually, his off-screen personality resembled his casting."[2] His most well known film was *Knute Rockne—All American*, in which Reagan played legendary football player George Gipp, who died two weeks after his final game. In a famous deathbed scene, the dying Gipp tells his coach, Knute Rockne, to "win just one for the Gipper"—a line Reagan would later use when campaigning.

Reagan also married his first wife, Jane Wyman, in 1940. They had a daughter, Maureen, in 1941, and adopted a son, Michael, in 1945. Reagan's career and his marriage, however, were interrupted by World War II. Reagan

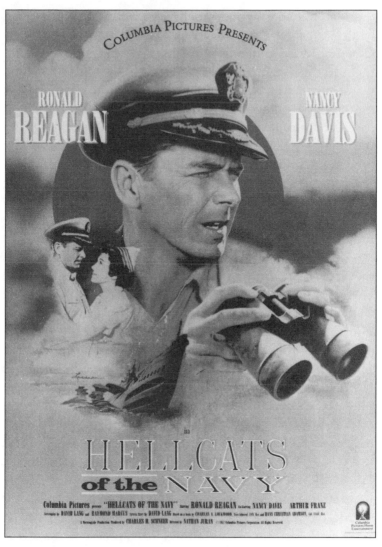

Ronald Reagan starred in fifty-three films before becoming president of the United States in 1980. In Hellcats of the Navy, *which debuted in 1957, Reagan co-starred with his second wife, Nancy Davis.*

was drafted, but because of poor eyesight was assigned to an Army Air Corps film unit based in Hollywood, where he helped produce inspirational films for the troops. When the war ended, Wyman's acting career was flourishing, while Reagan's never recovered. This reversal in their professional lives, coupled with other personal problems, led them to divorce in 1949.

"Reagan was also distracted from his career and his marriage by his work with the Screen Actors Guild (SAG),"[3] notes Pemberton. Initially Reagan helped fight to improve actor's pay and working conditions. After the war, however, with Hitler and the Nazi threat defeated, the Cold War began. Americans were concerned about the Soviet Union and the spread of communism, and SAG leaders became convinced that communists intended to infiltrate the movie industry in an attempt to brainwash Americans.

Reagan himself has written that before the war, he was a "bleeding-heart liberal" and had publicly supported Democratic politicians such as Harry S. Truman. After the war, however, Reagan's concerns about communism caused him to become more interested in politics and eventually adopt more conservative ideals. He wrote articles and made speeches denouncing communism, and he supported the House Un-American Activities Committee's efforts to purge Hollywood of communists by blacklisting left-wing actors. Reagan's passionate anticommunism would later define his foreign policy stance as president.

Reagan Enters Politics

In 1952 Ronald Reagan married actress Nancy Davis, and on March 4 of that year they had their first child, Patti. In 1954, with his film career fading, Reagan accepted a job as a host of and actor in the television program "General Electric Theater." For the next eight years he also visited GE plants throughout the country, making speeches to both factory workers and GE executives.

It was during this time that Reagan both completed the shift from anticommunist to full-fledged political conservative and honed the oratorical skills that served him well as a politician. As Schaller explains, "His several thousand after-dinner presentations invariably included an ode to 'traditional values,' an alarm about contemporary threats, and entertaining anecdotes. Year after year, Reagan warned of communism abroad and creeping socialism at home."[4] As his faith in business leaders and capitalism grew, he became opposed to high taxes and government regulation, convinced that they were barriers to economic growth. In denouncing Social Security and other "big government" programs, Reagan was effectively rejecting the ideals of the New Deal. Although he continued to admire Franklin D. Roosevelt as an inspirational leader, Reagan built his political career on attacking the expansion of government services that began under FDR.

Reagan's message matched that of an emerging new faction of the Republican Party. Loosely known as the "New Right," and led by Arizona senator Barry Goldwater, these Republicans urged a return to laissez-faire capitalism and warned against the Soviet threat. Goldwater ran for president in 1964, and Reagan campaigned for him. In an October 27, 1964, speech, Reagan denounced high taxes and expensive welfare programs and warned, "No government program ever voluntarily reduces itself in size. Government programs, once launched, never disappear."[5] Critics felt that this antigovernment message bred cynicism and undermined confidence in elected officials. Yet Reagan made his attack on government in profoundly optimistic terms: He spoke of America as God's shining "City on a Hill" and praised the power of individual Americans, whose potential he felt was constrained by government bureaucracy.

Lyndon Johnson beat Goldwater in a landslide victory, but Reagan's speeches had a powerful effect. A group of wealthy California Republicans decided to support Reagan in his 1966 run for governor of that state. "We realized that Reagan gave the Goldwater speech better than Goldwater,"[6] said one. Reagan defeated the incumbent Pat Brown and went on to serve two terms as governor. In office he continued his attack on welfare and other government programs. One of his favorite tactics was to tell anecdotes of "welfare cheats" who chose to take a government handout rather than work. Reagan succeeded in reducing welfare rolls but a Democratic legislature prevented him from enacting any radical changes in state policies.

Reagan's aspirations to the presidency initially met with failure. He sought the Republican nomination in 1968 and 1972, but lost twice to Richard Nixon. He came closer to beating Gerald Ford in the 1976 primaries, but the incumbent Ford won the nomination only to lose to Democrat Jimmy Carter in the presidential race. Undaunted by these defeats, Reagan began campaigning for the 1980 elections almost immediately, through a syndicated newspaper column and a daily radio commentary.

The 1980 Campaign

Reagan's success in the 1980 election was greatly facilitated by several problems that plagued the Carter presidency. The first was the economy. "The domestic economy was in shambles, plagued by an inflation rate exceeding 10 percent, an unemployment rate approaching 7 percent, federal budget deficits soaring past $40 billion annually and worsening trade deficits,"[7] explain historians John E. Findling and Frank W. Thackeray. While Carter certainly had not created these economic conditions, neither did he have a coherent plan for improving them.

In matters of foreign policy, Carter faced even worse problems. The Soviet Union invaded Afghanistan in December 1979, and this added fuel to conservatives' charges that Carter was soft on the Soviet Union. In response, Carter announced that the United States would institute economic sanctions against the Soviets and boycott the 1980 Olympics in Moscow, but this had little effect. Meanwhile, in November 1979, sixty-six Americans were captured by a militant Islamic group in Iran. Throughout 1980 Carter fought for their release, even ordering a military rescue mission, but his efforts were unsuccessful.

Historians Arthur S. Link, William A. Link, and William B. Catton note that "according to public opinion polls, Carter, during the summer of 1979, was the most unpopular president in modern history."[8] Reagan capitalized on Carter's failures, and in 1980 won 51 percent of the popular vote—compared to Carter's 41 percent—and captured 489 of the 538 electoral votes.

Reagan's Support of Supply-Side Economics

Reagan and his supporters interpreted their wide margin of victory as evidence of a popular mandate for change. During his campaign Reagan proclaimed "it's morning in America," implying that in the 1980s the nation would awake from the malaise of the 1970s. As if to support his claims, just twenty minutes after the new president and his running mate, George Bush, were sworn in on January 20, 1981, the hostages being held in Iran were released. Reagan entered the White House on a tremendous wave of popular support.

Yet Reagan faced all the same economic problems that Carter had. The new administration's approach to the economy rested on a theory known as supply-side economics. The keystone of supply-side theory was that if taxes are cut, incentives to work, save, and invest are increased. Supply-side economics also held that government expenditures must be reduced in proportion to the level at which taxes are cut, in order to achieve a balanced budget. Thus supply-side theory provided an economic rationale for Reagan's longtime political goals of cutting taxes and reducing the size of government.

Congress initially opposed the massive tax cuts Reagan called for, but the brewing controversy over his economic policies was temporarily interrupted on March 30, 1981. Just over two months after he was inaugurated, the president was shot and gravely wounded by would-be assassin John W. Hinckley Jr. Public support for the new president soared. (Later, when his public approval ratings plummeted after the Iran-contra affair, Reagan joked, "I could always get shot again."[9])

Shortly after his recovery, Reagan went before Congress and demanded that it pass his Economic Tax Recovery Act, which instituted a 25 percent reduction in income taxes over the next three years. With public support for the president so high, Congress acquiesced. Later Congress also passed the Tax Reform Act of 1986. Together these measures reduced the maximum federal income tax rate to less than half of what it had been before Reagan took office.

The economy lagged in recession for most of 1982, but Reagan remained optimistic, and in December 1982 the U.S. economy began an expansion—termed the "Reagan boom" by his supporters—that lasted the rest of the 1980s. In *The Reagan Effect: Economics and Presidential Leadership*, John W. Sloan notes:

> This period of growth lasted ninety-two months, more than twice the average length of expansions since World War II. By 1990, the gross national product (GNP) was 31 percent above the 1981 GNP in real, inflation-adjusted terms. Between 1982 and 1990, real disposable per capita income increased by 18 percent, and the economy added 18.4 million jobs.[10]

The Reagan Revolution

The booming economy no doubt contributed to Reagan's landslide reelection victory over Walter Mondale in 1984, which he won by the widest electoral margin in history. Many political commentators interpreted Reagan's enormous popularity, and the public's acceptance of his con-

Ronald Reagan's reelection victory over Walter Mondale in 1984 was a landslide. Reagan's enormous popularity and a booming economy contributed greatly to his success.

servative economics, as a sign that a national shift toward conservatism was underway. They termed the phenomenon the "Reagan Revolution," and continually compared Reagan to Franklin Roosevelt, the president who Reagan had long admired but whose New Deal Reagan sought to dismantle. "The American political system, during the presidency of Ronald Reagan, has been transformed to an extent unknown since the days of Franklin Delano Roosevelt,"[11] wrote John Chubb and Paul Peterson in their 1985 book *The New Direction in American Politics*. "Ronald Reagan's election to the presidency in 1980 marked the most decisive turning point in American history since the New Deal,"[12] according to Link, Link, and Catton.

Reagan's domestic policies, however, remain one of the most controversial aspects of his presidency. Critics charge that his tax cuts favored the rich and led to increased income inequality. "It was the truly wealthy, more than anyone else, who flourished under Reagan," writes Kevin

Phillips, author of *The Politics of Rich and Poor*, "the share of national income going to the wealthiest 1 percent rose from 8.1 percent in 1981 to 14.7 percent in 1986."[13] Reagan supporters are quick to address these claims. According to Sloan, "From the conservative point of view, the Reagan years were a period in which the rich got richer and the poor got richer. They frequently quoted John Kennedy's metaphor that a rising economic tide lifts all boats."[14]

But it is not just liberal Democrats who have taken issue with Reagan's domestic policies. Many conservatives have noted that, for all the talk of a "Reagan Revolution," large government programs such as Social Security, Medicare, and welfare were still largely intact when Reagan left office in 1989. "A significant shift in public policy, public opinion, and politics never happened in the 1980s,"[15] writes Larry M. Schwab in his book *The Illusion of a Conservative Reagan Revolution*. "The legacy of the 1981–1988 period was one of strengthening federal social programs rather than weakening them. . . . Not only did these programs survive, but their total budgets increased enormously during this period."[16]

Moreover, while Reagan failed to substantially cut federal social spending, he supported a massive increase in defense spending, which increased from $144 billion in 1980 to $290 billion in 1988. While the 1980s were a prosperous time for many Americans, notes historian Godfrey Hodgson, "this was achieved . . . at the cost of serious long-term damage to the economy."[17] Lower tax revenues and increased government spending added up to produce a budget deficit. The federal deficit averaged around $200 billion while Reagan was in office, and the national debt almost tripled, going from $1 trillion in 1981 to almost $3 trillion in 1989. With increased inequality and the national debt on the one hand, and the general prosperity of the 1980s on the other, economists continue to debate the overall Reagan economic legacy.

The Arms Race

Many of Reagan's supporters lament the budget deficits accrued under his administration but believe they were an unavoidable consequence of the Cold War. In this view, Reagan was torn between his domestic agenda of reducing government spending and his foreign policy goals. "If there was one single theme that had dominated Ronald Reagan's public pronouncements from 1947 until the end of his second term in office, it was his evangelical denunciation of communism, and his complete identification of American patriotism with anti-Sovietism,"[18] writes historian William H. Chafe. In a famous 1983 speech, he called the Soviet Union "the evil empire" and "the focus of evil in the modern world." Reagan rejected détente, Richard Nixon's policy of reducing tensions with Russia. Instead, he called for a "global campaign for freedom," that would "leave Marxism-Leninism on the ashheap of history."

Seeking to deal with the Soviet Union from a position of strength, Reagan brought about the greatest expansion of military power in American peacetime history. Under Carter, defense spending had increased by 5 percent a year; Reagan advanced it to 7 percent. Reagan reinstituted the plan to build the B-1 bomber that Carter had canceled, and also announced plans to build a new type of nuclear missile, the MX, or "peacekeeper" missile.

Reagan contended that the Soviet Union had pulled ahead in the arms race and that this military buildup was vital to national security. Critics disagreed, arguing that while the Soviet Union spent more on defense, the United States had more technologically sophisticated weaponry. Reagan's plan to deploy more nuclear missiles in Europe was particularly controversial, as peace advocates in both Europe and America held rallies calling for a "freeze" on nuclear deployment. In response to these pressures, Congress initially blocked funding for the MX missile, and defense spending remained an issue of contention between Reagan and Congress for most of his presidency.

The Strategic Defense Initiative

Yet despite his support of the arms race and his disdain of the nuclear freeze movement, Reagan himself abhorred nuclear weapons and believed they should be abolished completely—but only if both nations agreed. Reagan was alarmed to learn from intelligence advisers that the United States has no defense against a nuclear strike other than to launch its missiles in retaliation, and that only the prospect of mutually assured destruction prevents each nation from using its nuclear arsenal.

As Don Oberdorfer explains in *From the Cold War to a New Era: The United States and the Soviet Union, 1983–1991*, Reagan became "fascinated with the prospect of a technological breakthrough that would create hardware that could stop incoming missiles. Reagan often called the idea 'my dream.'"[19] In 1983, in a nationally televised address, Reagan announced plans to make his "dream," a satellite system that would shoot down nuclear missiles before they reached their targets, a reality. The system was called the Strategic Defense Initiative (SDI), and because it was to be space-based, the media quickly dubbed it the "Star Wars" missile defense system.

Like the rest of his foreign policy, SDI was highly controversial. To many, including several top Soviet officials, it seemed like Reagan was preparing the United States for nuclear war. Other critics charged that building a defense against nuclear missiles would be impossible, and in fact no SDI satellites were ever produced. Reagan's defenders, however, view SDI as one of the president's greatest decisions. Because SDI would be enormously expensive, any Soviet attempt to match it would be a further drain on their already weakening economy. National Security Adviser Robert McFarlane later claimed that SDI was adopted for the purpose of bankrupting the Soviet Union. Thus Reagan's supporters view SDI as the centerpiece of a strategy to win the arms race, and eventually bring the Cold War to an end, by outspending the Soviets.

The Reagan Doctrine and the Iran-Contra Affair

In addition to the arms race, the Reagan administration supported the efforts of some Third World governments in Africa and Central America that were fighting communism. "The Reagan Doctrine," as this policy is known, was controversial because it sometimes meant that the United States sent military aid to noncommunist but nevertheless authoritarian dictatorships suspected of human rights abuses. This was the case with U.S. support for the government of El Salvador in its fight to suppress the National Liberation Front, a rebel group that was receiving aid from Cuba and the Soviet Union.

During Reagan's second term, the controversy surrounding U.S. involvement in Central America contributed to the worst scandal of his presidency, the Iran-contra affair. The affair began with the Reagan administration's efforts to gain the release of hostages being held in Iran. In violation of U.S. policy, officials in the White House authorized the sale of weapons to groups in Iran who were believed to have influence with the terrorists. Later, to the administration's dismay, it was revealed that these arms were going almost directly to the terrorists themselves, and that the terrorists were taking new hostages for those they released. Complicating matters, some of the funds derived from the sale of weapons to Iran were diverted to aid the contras, a rebel group fighting the Communist government of Nicaragua.

While the "Iran" part of the Iran-contra affair was shocking, from a legal perspective the covert funding of the contras was more troubling. "Public opinion polls revealed much popular opposition to American military involvement in Central America, and fears of being drawn into another Vietnam-like quagmire,"[20] explains historian George Moss. Because of this, Congress passed the Boland amendment in 1982, forbidding any further CIA or Department of Defense funding of the contras. When the Reagan administration then funded the contras through the National Security Agency, Congress passed "Boland II" to close this loophole. Thus while the sale of weapons to Iran could be attributed to poor intelligence about the groups in Iran or simply to poor judgment by the Reagan officials, the continued funding of the contras was specifically prohibited by U.S. law. The Reagan administration had pursued its own foreign policy goals, in direct violation of Congress.

The events of the Iran-contra affair, after they were revealed in late 1986, spawned two congressional investigations and the appointment of an independent counsel to investigate possible criminal wrongdoing by White House officials. While all three investigations concluded that Reagan was ultimately responsible for the Iran-contra scandal, they stopped short of accusing the president of any crime. Nevertheless, Iran-contra had hurt Reagan politically. Moss writes that "one of the most popular and successful presidents of modern times, who had enjoyed remarkably smooth sailing through his first six years, faced much stormy political weather for the rest of his presidency."[21] Moreover, the Iran-contra affair overshadowed what have since come to be regarded as some of Reagan's greatest achievements: his meetings with Soviet leader Mikhail Gorbachev.

Reagan and Gorbachev

There was a succession of Soviet leaders during Reagan's first term in office. In 1982, Leonid Brezhnev died and was replaced by Yuri Andropov. Constantin Chernenko came to power when Andropov died in early 1984, but the 73-year-old Chernenko ruled for only 390 days before he also passed away. Then on March 11, 1985, the Politburo elected a younger and more vigorous man, Mikhail Gorbachev, to lead the Soviet Union.

Gorbachev was convinced that the Soviet government had become corrupt and its economy stagnant and inefficient. As part of his program for reform, Gorbachev advocated *glasnost*, the Russian word for *openness*, in both the Soviet Union itself and its relations with the West. Gorbachev would later be viewed as a revolutionary by both Soviet and Western observers, but at the time no one anticipated that Gorbachev's reforms would lead to collapse of the Soviet Union in 1991.

Still, the new Russian leader did make some bold moves in 1985. Just a month after his election, Gorbachev announced that the Soviets would halt nuclear testing and the deployment of intermediate-range missiles. Reagan had not met with any Soviet leader during his first term, but recognized that Gorbachev was very different from his predecessors. "In October 1985, calling for a 'fresh start' in U.S.-Soviet relations, Reagan told his cabinet to suspend the use of such terms as 'evil empire,'"[22] writes professor of history Wesley M. Bagby. In November of that year the two leaders met for the first time in Geneva, Switzerland.

At their first summit meeting Reagan and Gorbachev quarreled over the arms race, SDI, and each nation's involvement in Central America. However, both expressed an interest in arms control, and Reagan's "fresh start" took his public approval ratings to new heights. "The public that elected Reagan as a cold warrior applauded him as a peacemaker,"[23] notes Schaller. When they met for the second time in October 1986 at Reykjavik, Iceland, the atmosphere was extraordinarily optimistic. As Bagby explains:

> They agreed to total elimination within ten years of all Soviet and U.S. intermediate-range missiles in Europe (the "zero option"). Reagan proposed that they eliminate all ballistic missiles, and Gorbachev proposed elim-

inating all nuclear weapons, to which Reagan replied "that suits me fine." For a moment the world seemed close to agreement on nuclear disarmament, a prospect that [Secretary of State George] Schultz called "breathtaking." But then, when an elated Reagan thought they had agreed on everything, Gorbachev insisted that all depended "on your giving up SDI." Enraged, Reagan "blew my top" and "walked out on Gorbachev."[24]

"After having soared so far toward a common vision of a demilitarized future, only to plummet to earth in the final hour,"[25] writes Oberdorfer, Reykjavik was an enormous disappointment for Reagan. And it was followed just weeks later by the first reports of the Iran-contra affair. The administration lived under the cloud of Iran-contra for much of 1987, but in December of that year Reagan again met with Gorbachev in Washington, D.C. In what became known as "the second zero," the Soviets had agreed to abolish intermediate-range nuclear weapons, regardless of America's commitment to SDI (perhaps because the Soviets guessed that American researchers had made little progress on the program). At the Washington summit the two signed the Intermediate-Range Nuclear Forces (INF) Treaty, with each nation agreeing to destroy all their missiles of that type.

Reagan and Gorbachev met for one final summit meeting in May 1988, this time with Reagan paying a visit to Moscow. Though none of the agreements reached there were as sweeping as the INF treaty, the images of the two leaders shaking hands in Red Square would have been unthinkable to most Americans in 1980. U.S.-Soviet relations essentially hit an all-time high at the Moscow summit; soon after it the Soviet Union would face a number of crises.

The Collapse of the Soviet Union

Gorbachev had initiated economic reforms known as *perestroika*, the Russian word for *restructuring*, and criticized

Russian President Mikhail Gorbachev and President Reagan sign the Intermediate-Range Nuclear Forces (INF) Treaty in December 1987. Under the treaty each nation agreed to destroy all of their intermediate-range nuclear missiles.

the *nomenklatura*, the Soviet ruling class. Yet his actions had unintended consequences in the satellite nations of Eastern Europe that had been under Soviet control for decades. Joseph Smith writes, "The introduction of *glasnost* and *perestroika* in the Soviet Union stimulated movements for the same fundamental reforms in Eastern Europe. In the process, the power and authority of local communist bosses were seriously challenged and swept away."[26]

One by one, anticommunist movements arose within Poland, Hungary, Czechoslovakia, Bulgaria, East Germany, and Romania. Unlike his predecessors, Gorbachev did not use force to suppress these movements, but these nations rejected communism more quickly than he expected. The sudden, spontaneous nature of the revolutions of 1989 was captured on November 9, 1989, when East Germany opened the Berlin Wall and it was subsequently torn down by jubilant crowds. Prodemocracy movements in Russia itself, coupled with the economic problems of the Soviet economy, finally led to the disintegration of the Soviet Union into its constituent republics in 1991, marking a formal end of the Cold War.

By that time, of course, President Reagan left office and his former vice president, George Bush, succeeded him. But it is Reagan who is often credited for ending the Cold War. His supporters argue that the military buildup of the early 1980s helped bankrupt the Soviet economy. However, as with so much of Reagan's legacy, this claim is controversial. Many observers hold that the economic problems plaguing the Soviet Union when Gorbachev came to power were the result of decades of inefficient state control of the economy rather than a result of the Reagan arms buildup. In this view, Reagan's support of the arms race was dangerous, expensive, and unnecessary.

A Controversial President

These various explanations for how Reagan may or may not have helped bring about the collapse of the Soviet Union came only after he had left office. In January 1989, as he was about to leave office, the media made yet another comparison between Ronald Reagan and Franklin D. Roosevelt. The Gallup Poll reported that Reagan had received the highest public approval rating on leaving office than any president since FDR.

Statistics such as this, in addition to his landslide victory in the 1984 election and his ability to survive a political disaster as big as the Iran-contra affair, have contributed to the aura surrounding Reagan's popularity. His admirers attributed the public fascination with Reagan to his charisma, and dubbed him "the Great Communicator." A less flattering nickname was the "Teflon president," given to him because, like the cookware of the same name, nothing bad seemed to stick to him.

Thus even Reagan's popularity was, and remains, a controversial topic. Just as with his economic policies, his dealings with the Soviet Union, and his role in the Iran-contra affair, there are two conflicting schools of thought on Ronald Reagan's speechmaking abilities. Conservatives call him an inspirational leader; liberals call him a demagogue. Admirers believe he had a gift for communicating with the public; critics suspect he was just an actor reading lines.

The reason for all the controversy over Reagan, writes California State University professor of political science Mark T. Clark, is that "the political debate over his presidency still inhibits objective scholarship of his legacy.... Not until we move further away from the political issues that defined the 1980s will a more balanced and complete picture emerge."[27] Democrats generally opposed Reagan's attack on "big government," so they hesitate to give the former president any favorable remarks. Republicans, on the other hand, are unlikely to be very critical of one of the most popular candidates their party ever produced, and some often describe the Reagan years in very idealistic terms.

These biased accounts of the Reagan presidency make objective historical analysis more difficult, but the recentness of Reagan's presidency also inhibits historical study in other ways. Many of the documents pertaining to the Cold War, for example, are still classified. Yet while it is true that historical hindsight and new information will help give a more complete picture of Reagan, the current debates over the former president's policies already reveal a great deal about the effect he has had on American politics. Even clearly biased accounts of Reagan's tax cuts, for example, are fascinating because they show how political commentators often interpret the same series of events in completely different ways.

Life After the Presidency

In *President Reagan: The Role of a Lifetime*, journalist Lou Cannon gives a detailed account of Reagan's last day in office. He describes the president as eager to resume a more carefree life on his ranch in Santa Barbara, California. "An aide, thinking about it later, would say that Reagan had made fifty-three movies and that being on a movie set was like being cooped up in the White House with your crew all those years. Reagan was ready for the freedom of California and a new role."[28]

Seventy-seven years old when he left office in January 1989, Reagan was the oldest person ever to have served as president. In November 1994 he announced he had Alzheimer's disease, and since then has been largely out of the public eye. In November 1991, the Ronald Reagan Presidential Library and Museum, part of the presidential libraries system administered by the National Archives and Record Administration, opened in Simi Valley, California, to aid in the continuing study of Reagan's policies and legacy.

Notes

1. William E. Pemberton, *Exit with Honor: The Life and Presidency of Ronald Reagan*. New York: M.E. Shape, 1997, p. 7.
2. Michael Schaller, *Reckoning with Reagan: America and Its President in the 1980s*. New York: Oxford University Press, 1992, p. 7.
3. Pemberton, *Exit with Honor*, p. 28.
4. Schaller, *Reckoning with Reagan*, p. 10.
5. Ronald Reagan, Televised National Address on Behalf of Senator Barry Goldwater, October 27, 1964, quoted in Ronald Reagan, ed., *Speaking My Mind: Selected Speeches*. New York: Simon and Schuster, 1989, p. 32.
6. Quoted in Pemberton, *Exit with Honor*, p. 64.
7. John E. Findling and Frank W. Thackeray, eds., *Events That Changed America in the Twentieth Century*. Westport, CT: Greenwood Press, 1996, p. 191.
8. Arthur S. Link, William A. Link, and William B. Catton, *American Epoch: A History of the United States Since 1900, Volume II: An Era of War and Uncertain Peace 1936–1985*. New York: Alfred A. Knopf, 1987, p. 654.
9. Quoted in Dinesh D'Souza, *Ronald Reagan: How an Ordinary Man Became an Extraordinary Leader*. New York: Free Press, 1997, p. 229.
10. John W. Sloan, *The Reagan Effect: Economics and Presidential Leadership*. Lawrence: University of Kansas Press, 1999, p. 7.

11. Quoted in Larry M. Schwab, *The Illusion of a Conservative Reagan Revolution*. New Brunswick, NJ: Transaction, 1991, p. 2.

12. Link, Link, and Catton, *American Epoch*, p. 654.

13. Kevin Phillips, "Reagan's America: A Capital Offense," *New York Times Magazine*, June 17, 1990, p. 26.

14. Sloan, *The Reagan Effect*, p. 7.

15. Schwab, *The Illusion of a Conservative Reagan Revolution*, p. 15.

16. Schwab, *The Illusion of a Conservative Reagan Revolution*, p. 12.

17. Godfrey Hodgson, *The World Turned Right Side Up: A History of the Conservative Ascendancy in America*. Boston: Houghton Mifflin, 1996, p. 256.

18. William H. Chafe, *The Unfinished Journey: America Since World War II*. New York: Oxford University Press, 1991, p. 491.

19. Don Oberdorfer, *From the Cold War to a New Era: The United States and the Soviet Union, 1983–1991*. Baltimore: Johns Hopkins University Press, 1998, p. 25.

20. George Moss, *America in the Twentieth Century*. Englewood Cliffs, NJ: Prentice-Hall, 1989, p. 442.

21. Moss, *America in the Twentieth Century*, p. 454.

22. Wesley M. Bagby, *America's International Relations Since World War I*. New York: Oxford University Press, 1999, p. 350.

23. Schaller, *Reckoning with Reagan*, p. 120.

24. Bagby, *America's International Relations Since World War I*, pp. 351–52.

25. Oberdorfer, *From the Cold War to a New Era*, p. 205.

26. Smith, *The Cold War*, p. 141.

27. Mark T. Clark, "The Reagan Legacy Up for Grabs," *Current*, July/August 1999, p. 34.

28. Lou Cannon, *President Reagan: The Role of a Lifetime*. New York: Simon and Schuster, 1991, p. 15.

PRESIDENTS *and their* DECISIONS

CHAPTER

1

Reaganomics

THE REAGAN PRESIDENCY CONSTITUTED A PROFOUND CHANGE IN U.S. POLITICS

DAVID MERVIN

In the 1930s the federal government instituted a large number of programs, such as Social Security, designed to help people recover from the Great Depression. Franklin D. Roosevelt dubbed this package of programs the New Deal, and since then that term has often been used to describe the overall belief that the government has a legitimate role in dealing with social problems such as poverty and health care.

Ronald Reagan, however, believed that New Deal–style policies and big government were harming America. In his first inaugural address, he proclaimed, "Government is not the solution to our problem; government is the problem." The Reagan administration favored reducing taxes and lowering spending on programs such as welfare. Since Reagan was the first president to openly oppose policies of the New Deal, many commentators hailed his election in 1981 as the "Reagan Revolution," and predicted a profound shift in American politics toward more conservative ideals of limited government. In the following excerpt from his book *Ronald Reagan and the American Presidency*, David Mervin contends that although Reagan was unable to implement many of his goals, the president did preside over the emergence of a "new public philosophy" under which excessive government spending and liberal ideology are no longer the dominant themes in American politics. Mervin is a senior lecturer in politics at the University of Warwick in Great Britain.

WHEN HE FIRST ENTERED THE WHITE HOUSE REAGAN'S principal objectives were to reduce the size and role of government, to reinvigorate the economy and to strengthen the nation's defences. In pursuit of those aims Reagan sought policy change aimed at increasing defence expenditure, cutting taxes and curtailing domestic programmes. Broadly speaking, Reagan achieved these ambitious ends.

> Even critics must admit that a determined president was able to accomplish many of his stated goals. Reagan gained the largest increase in peace time defense spending, a step he felt was necessary in order for the country to regain its position as the world's preeminent military power. Reagan cut tax rates sharply and dramatically altered the income tax system, policies to which his administration was also deeply committed. Reagan sheared back a great number of domestic programs, thus carrying out in good part his promises to reduce the scope of the domestic side of government.[1]

Inevitably Reagan enjoyed only partial success in translating his objectives into policy change. In particular, the reductions in domestic expenditure were far more modest than were necessary to prevent ballooning budget deficits, given the reductions in tax revenue and the increases in defence spending. Reagan failed spectacularly to deliver his 1980 campaign promise to balance the budget; large budget deficits and an enormous national debt are part of the legacy of Reaganomics. Budget deficits—in constant dollars (1982)—averaged $161 billion for the first six years of the Reagan administration as compared to an annual average of $28 billion since 1950. The national debt, meanwhile, tripled during the Reagan years to more than $2.6 trillion. . . .

Perversely, however, deficits made a major contribution to Reagan's central purpose of limiting government. Everyone agreed that deficits were bad and should be reduced as soon as possible, but to do so by increasing taxes was unacceptable to the majority of Americans. In this context, liberal Democrats in congress were forced on to the defensive. The revenue was not available to support the programmes that they might otherwise have advanced to deal with various pressing social problems. 'The federal budget deficit makes it impossible for Democrats to talk about any major new domestic spending programs unless they also talk about raising taxes. Which is exactly what the Republicans want them to talk about.'[2] Budget deficits coupled with tax cuts helped Reagan to bring about a fundamental change of ethos in the United States, one where extensions of the role of the federal government were no longer acceptable.

Reagan's Resoluteness

In his final television address to the nation in January 1989 the president asserted, 'We weren't just marking time, we made a difference.' This undeniable claim summarizes the single most important accomplishment of the Reagan administration. United States domestic and foreign policies were significantly different under Reagan than they had been before. So many presidents come and go without bringing about such change. They may compile respectable legislative records; they may even have more impressive *Congressional Quarterly* presidential support scores than Reagan, but the overall effect of their having been in office has been slight—they were 'just marking time'.

Repeatedly, presidents have gone to Washington declaring their intention to move the country in this or that direction, insisting that they would bring about real change. Typically such promises have remained undelivered; in almost all cases the realities of office have forced presidents to lower their sights and to settle for keeping the machinery of government ticking over rather than trying to bring about major alterations in direction. As James

MacGregor Burns noted, the pundits fully expected Reagan to follow a similar path:

> Had not Eisenhower departed from his 1952 rhetoric to embrace most of the New Deal program? Had not both Richard Nixon and Jerry Ford moved from the right or moderate right wing of the GOP to its center. Democrats had done the same . . . only in the opposite direction. Both John Kennedy and Jimmy Carter had entered office as 'rhetorical radicals' and soon turned into fiscal moderates.

Within weeks of George Bush taking office, the press was to be found reporting evidence of the new president distancing himself from the conservative programme on which he was elected and moving towards the ideological centre.

Irrespective of widespread popular impressions, Ronald Reagan proved to be far more resolute than most other presidents. He, too, fell a long way short of his original objectives. Many compromises were necessary and he suffered some considerable reverses in attempting to gain acceptance of his policies. It is also the case that almost all of Reagan's great legislative triumphs occurred at the beginning of his first term. Nevertheless despite the qualifications and the setbacks, taken as a whole, the effect of Reagan's tenure was to bring about policy change of a sort that had not been seen in the United States for half a century. 'He was a strong president and imposed his policies on the country,' James Sundquist commented. 'He turned the whole trend of American government around. We were headed in the direction of the welfare state and all Republicans could do before was to slow the trend. Reagan halted it.' In the same vein Louis Harris has said,

> Eisenhower, Nixon and Ford had been conservative on many issues. But they all had one characteristic in common that Ronald Reagan did not share; none of them had the daring to assault the federal government as the

last haven for help in solving social ills. All tacitly assumed that the basic thrust of the New Deal would remain intact. None dared to make the federal government an object of attack, as the root of most of the evil.

Unlike other Republican presidents, Reagan was prepared to challenge directly the assumptions upon which the New Deal was based. He failed to bring about a revolution or an electoral realignment and he certainly was not able to dismantle the New Deal. What Reagan did was to provide the leadership necessary for a change in the terms of debate; he presided over the emergence of a new public philosophy.

Challenging the New Deal

A public philosophy has been briefly defined as 'the outlook on public affairs that seems to be taken for granted in a particular period'.[3] Thus, in the first decade or so of the twentieth century a consensus developed behind progressive notions of political and economic reform; progressivism permeated mass and élite thinking, was embraced by both political parties and thereby took on the form of a new public philosophy. Similarly, in the 1930s, a body of ideas evolved in support of the New Deal providing an intellectual underpinning for Roosevelt's policies and his theory of governance. Not everyone, but certainly a vast majority of Americans, came to accept that the presidency should, in peace or war, be the main focus and the principal initiator in the federal government. It was widely accepted that the problems and complexities of modern society could no longer be left to the vagaries of market forces and the ministrations of local and state governments; social and economic ills had to be addressed by the federal government in Washington.

For close to half a century before Reagan became president, the public philosophy of the New Deal dominated American politics. Journalists, voters and politicians of

Reagan vs. Roosevelt

Historians often compare Ronald Reagan with Franklin Delano Roosevelt. Both presidents were popular, charismatic leaders who advocated controversial political agendas. In his book The Unfinished Journey: America Since World War II, *historian William H. Chafe notes the irony of the comparison: While Reagan looked up to Roosevelt, he nevertheless advocated a complete reversal of FDR's New Deal policies.*

To a degree unmatched in any era since Franklin Roosevelt's New Deal, Ronald Reagan imprinted his personal brand on the decade of the 1980s.... The country was in trouble, he believed, let down by leaders too prone to worry about nagging dilemmas, too obsessed with limits rather than possibilities. And so the voters "rounded up a posse, swore in this old sheriff, and sent us riding into town." In those words, Ronald Reagan described how he defined his presidential role—to rescue America, restore confidence, and sweep away all the doubters

both parties had taken as given the assumptions upon which it was based. Its staying power was apparently demonstrated in 1964 when Barry Goldwater, the Republican candidate for the presidency and an openly declared foe of the New Deal, went down to crushing defeat. On the other hand, more prudent conservative Republicans such as Eisenhower and Nixon avoided head-on collisions with the New Deal, doing no more than seeking 'to slow the trend'.

Reagan was no less a radical conservative than Goldwater, but an infinitely more skilful political leader. While many Americans had found Goldwater to be a rather frightening figure who just might abolish social security and precipitate World War III, the smiling, non-threatening image

and skeptics who insisted on talking about "problems."

Appropriately enough, Reagan came to the White House determined to emulate Franklin Roosevelt, his only real political hero. His generation too, Reagan said, "had a rendezvous with destiny." In simple phrases reminiscent of FDR, Reagan spoke of America "standing tall" once again, overcoming fear and insecurity, winning the "big ones" for the good side—except that Reagan's goal was to dismantle the institutional legacy of his hero, and to use the commanding power of the presidency to undermine the welfare state. Thus, while paying lip service to his hero, Reagan excoriated the Great Society, denounced environmentalists, condemned welfare recipients as too "lazy" to get a job, and lambasted the Soviet Union as an "evil empire." More to the point, he acted on these pronouncements, and, to a degree that astonished even his closest allies, succeeded in getting his way.

William H. Chafe, *The Unfinished Journey: America Since World War II.* New York: Oxford University Press, 1991.

projected by Reagan was far more reassuring. Yet beneath the mask of affability, there was a man of uncommon resolution intent on replacing the New Deal with Reaganism.

Reagan enjoyed only mixed success in translating his intentions into policy change. Federal programmes were cut and eliminated, but far fewer than had been hoped for. Devolution to the states did occur, but again the achievement fell short of the goal. Big cuts in taxation did take place, but the reductions in federal expenditure were insufficient to make balancing the budget possible. A limited degree of deregulation did take place and the Pentagon entered a new era of plenty. This is a limited, uneven and yet impressive record. It is not impressive, of course, if measured against some abstract model of executive leadership, or if judged in terms appropriate to Mrs. Thatcher. But, if properly placed in context, it represents a level of achievement superior to that of most White House incumbents.

Democrats Have Adopted Reaganite Assumptions

In gaining partial acceptance of his programme, Reagan was instrumental in the creation of a new public philosophy. The evidence for that is best seen in the extent to which Democratic candidates and elected officials came to accept Reaganite assumptions. This was apparent in the 1984 election when the president's

> steadfast support of across-the-board tax cuts in the face of intense pressure from established opinion led his Democratic party opponent, Walter Mondale, to make the achievement of a balanced budget into a positive moral virtue. Thus a Republican issue . . . became the mainstay of Democratic speeches and advertisements. . . . Virtually nothing was heard from the Democratic party about social welfare. Hardly a peep sounded in regard to a massive jobs program . . . [Reagan] shifted the entire debate in an economically conservative direction.[4]

In the 1980s liberal Democrats in the national legislature, the keepers of the New Deal grail, 'had to accommodate the widespread view that the government cannot afford major new domestic expenditures and that public support is flagging for the kind of government programs that were a key tool of Great Society liberalism'.[5] As Henry Waxman, a liberal Democratic congressman from California, ruefully explained, 'It's disappointing and frustrating. We're not doing what we ought to be doing. The liberal agenda is fighting to keep what we have.' The terms of the debate had clearly changed; liberals were reduced to damage limitation exercises and rearguard actions. They could do little more than fend off the worst excesses of programme cutting by the administration. As Waxman put it, 'I have to look at stopping the Reagan Administration from gutting the Clean Air Act as one of the great successes, and salvaging many of the health programs as an accomplishment.'

In the 1988 national elections there was ample evidence of Democrats taking to the wearing of Reaganite clothes. Dukakis set his face against any reversal of Reagan's tax cuts either as a way of cutting the deficit or of financing new programmes and 'the extent to which the prevailing Democratic philosophy incorporates elements of Reaganomics' was widely commented upon.[6] As *Time* magazine noted after Bush's nomination:

> At the very least [the President] has defined the debate. Opinion polls show some vague unease about the economy's future, along with renewed interest in federal solutions for a variety of social ills. Still, Reagan's preachments about the evils of Big Government and high progressive tax rates continue to dominate the political landscape. Even his failures, the most monumental being the nation's mounting debt, have served to constrain the discussion.

It was with more than a little justification that Martin Anderson boasted, 'What Reagan and his comrades have done is to shape America's policy agenda well into the twenty-first century. The prospects are nil for sharply progressive tax rates and big, new social welfare programs, some of the former mainstays of the Democrats domestic policy agenda. Everyone is for a strong national defense, differing only in the degree and quality of it.'

A situation that was a source of great satisfaction to a conservative like Anderson was a cause for bitter regret to Democratic Senator Ernest Hollings. Although a trenchant critic of Reagan's domestic policy, Hollings, unlike some other liberals, was enough of a realist to recognize how successful the former president was in gaining his objectives:

> When Ronald Reagan came to Washington in 1981, he
> made no bones about his intention to slash government
> spending and trash the federal bureaucracy. He flaunt-
> ed his contempt for government. Eight years later liber-
> al pundits crow that the Reagan Revolution has failed,
> that the federal fortress stands stronger than ever. They
> are dead wrong. The reality is that President Reagan
> dealt Uncle Sam a crippling blow. He left a federal trea-
> sury that is paralysed by debt; a federal work force that
> is demoralized and discredited; a public infrastructure
> that is literally crumbling. What's more by mobilizing
> the nation's voters as 'an overpowering bloc vote against
> necessary taxation' (David Stockman's words), Reagan
> sapped the government's capacity to put its house—and
> books—in order.

Reducing the Role of Government

Hollings goes on to identify a few of the areas of public policy where evidence of 'the demise of government' that Reagan sought can be found. The Reagan administration failed
in its aim of abolishing the Department of Education, but
reduced its staff by a quarter and cut its programmes sav-
agely. Education block grants to the states were reduced by
63 per cent; grants for bilingual education were cut by 47
per cent; for vocational education by 29 per cent and for
college work study by 26.5 per cent. Federal funding for
subsidized housing was cut by 81 per cent during the Reagan years. The level of benefits and the range of coverage
was reduced for 'safety net' programmes like Aid to Families
with Dependent Children. In 1978, 3 per cent of the federal
budget was devoted to natural resources, environmental
protection and conservation programmes whereas by 1988
that percentage was halved. In those few areas of public policy not immune to cutting, Reagan had 'made a difference'
even if it was a difference that liberals like Hollins deplored.

Reagan's policies also had significant consequences for federalism in the United States. Like other Republican incumbents he was troubled by the seemingly incessant growth of the national government in Washington at the expense of the states since the 1930s. Eisenhower and Nixon had sought to redress the balance by devolving federal responsibilities to state and local governments. For them bringing government closer to the people was a desirable end in itself as well as a means of providing for a more efficient and effective delivery of services. Reagan's approach was far more radical in its implications; he too was wedded to the federal ideal, but this was of secondary importance compared to his primary purpose of substantially reducing the role of government *per se*. As he said in his first inaugural address,

> Government is not the solution to our problem; government is the problem. . . . It is time to check and reverse the growth of government. . . . It is my intention to curb the size and influence of the federal establishment and to demand recognition of the distinction between the powers granted to the federal government and those reserved to the states or to the people.

In some respects Reagan's actions fell far short of this statement of intention. Total civilian employment in the federal government in fact rose by 3 per cent from 1980–1987. Much of this increase is explained by the shift of priorities towards defence, an area of government activity where civilian employment grew by 11.5 per cent in the same period, but even non defence federal civilian employment only declined by 1.4 per cent.

It is also the case that total federal budget outlays (measured in constant 1982 dollars) increased from $699.1 billion in 1980 to $859.3 billion in 1987 and even non defence federal budget outlays increased from $535.1 billion to $609.5 billion in the same period. However the increases in

federal domestic expenditures 1980–87 are partly account-
ed for by payments to individuals and the interest payments incurred by the large deficits of the Reagan years.

A more favourable picture of Reagan's effectiveness in
achieving his goal of limiting the scope of government can
be derived from statistics concerned with federal aid to
state and local government. During the 1970s such aid had
risen steeply increasing annually by an average of 14.43 per
cent. By contrast, Reagan succeeded in sharply reducing
the rate of increase and actually brought about declines in
1982 and 1987. It should also be noted that federal grants-
in-aid as a percentage of total federal outlays declined from
15.5 per cent to 10.8 per cent between 1980 and 1987.
Meanwhile federal grants as a percentage of state and local
government outlays dropped from 25.8 per cent to 18.2
per cent; similarly, during the same period, federal aid as a
percentage of GNP fell from 3.4 per cent to 2.5 per cent.
Once again Reagan's record was uneven, but there is no
doubt that he had an impact on the relationship between
the federal government and the states that few other presidents have been able to equal.

Notes

1. Paul Peterson and Mark Rom, 'Lower Taxes, More Spending and
   Budget Deficits' in Jones, *The Reagan Legacy*, op. cit., pp. 213–40.
2. William Schneider in 'The Political Legacy of the Reagan Years' in
   Sidney Blumenthal and Thomas Byrne Edsall (eds), *The Reagan
   Legacy*. Pantheon Books, New York 1988, pp. 51–98.
3. Hugh Heclo, 'Reaganism and the Search for a Public Philosophy',
   in Palmer, *Perspectives on the Reagan Years*, op. cit., pp. 31–63.
4. Aaron Wildavsky, 'President Reagan as Political Strategist', *Society*
   (May/June), pp. 56–62.
5. Janet Hook, 'Liberal Democrats Adapt to a Hostile Climate', *Congressional Quarterly Weekly Report* (9 Aug. 1986), pp. 1797–801.
6. David Broder, 'The Democrats Together At Last', *The Washington
   Post*, National Weekly Edition, (18–24 July 1988), p. 6.

Reaganomics Was a Success

Esmond Wright

Reagan was a strong advocate of supply-side economics, so much so that the press dubbed the economic theory "Reaganomics." As Esmond Wright explains in the following excerpt from his book *The American Dream: From Reconstruction to Reagan*, supply-side economics was based largely on George Gilder's book *Wealth and Poverty*, which argued that government regulation of the economy is detrimental, and on the ideas of Arthur Laffer, who believed that high taxes hurt the economy and thereby reduced overall government revenue. Based on these theories, the Reagan administration worked to reduce the size of the federal government and to cut taxes.

Wright, a professor of history at the University of London, maintains that Reagan's economic policies helped initiate the largest surge in the U.S. economy since World War II, what he terms the "Reagan boom." He details the economic leaps that America made during the 1980s and argues that Reagan's 1981 Economic Recovery Tax Act helped stimulate this growth and helped all Americans, not just the very rich, to become more prosperous.

THERE WAS ANOTHER FACTOR ALONGSIDE A STRONG foreign-policy stance to which Reagan attributed his success in national politics: his advocacy of supply-side economics and tax cuts. It fitted in with his own optimistic upbeat view of America if only the energies of the ordinary

Excerpted from Esmond Wright, *The American Dream: From Reconstruction to Reagan*. Copyright © Esmond Wright 1996. Reprinted by permission of Blackwell Publishers Ltd.

American people could be released, then they could overcome the problems that the United States faced. He was impressed that most of the conservative journals that he read—such as *National Review* or *Human Events*—were endorsing these ideas. In origin the ideas of Frederick Hayek, who for a time taught in Chicago, and of Milton Friedman became the language of Thatcherism, and formed the fashionable doctrines both in Britain and the US: the only way to enhance the performance of the economy was to improve its supply-side, by greater efficiency, to make markets better, to reduce costs and to increase competitiveness. It became increasingly clear that these were popular ideas with the electorate, which would gain Reagan votes in his campaign for the presidency. Once he had grasped this idea, he then became the Great Communicator of supply-side economics to a wider audience. . . .

The President sought also to cut the size of government itself. By promising cuts in his defense program the President hoped to reduce the awesome figures of the federal budget deficit. The size of the government deficit, and the political difficulties of reducing it, however, ensured that once private and credit demand was added to the government's needs, interest rates were bound to rise. Interest rates stayed stubbornly high (10 percent against 20 percent in 1980), attracting short-term outside and mobile capital but delaying business revival. As a result unemployment stayed high, at 8.4 percent (though this was the lowest for two years). It was especially burdensome in some areas (for instance, the Middle West), among 16–24-year-olds, and among blacks. And there was (and remains) for the US, as for some British banks, a high exposure to Latin American debt problems.

The New Economic Theology

In keeping with the fashion set by the White House, the new economic theology even had overtones of the Gilded Age. Much more overtly than the supply-siders and the anti-tax theorists, Law and Economics stalwarts flirted with a neo-Darwinism that echoed Herbert Spencer and William Graham Sumner in its view that commercial selection processes in the market place could largely displace government decision-making. One intellectual frontiersman, Richard Posner, University of Chicago law professor turned federal appeals judge, even briefly suggested making a market for babies so it would be easier for couples to adopt. A second prominent Chicago legalist, Richard A. Epstein, leader of the movement's "economic rights" faction, deplored most government economic regulation as unconstitutional. "I oppose most of the legislation written in this century," he acknowledged in 1987. Posner and Epstein defined a remote ideological periphery, but they also confirmed the power of the mainstream conservative resurgence.

Most of the conservative theorists acknowledged their restatement of Adam Smith. The most important—and popular—of the theorists was George Gilder, in his *Wealth and Poverty*. Gilder wrote what stands as the comprehensive theology of the Reagan era, relating conservatism to five central objectives. First was the importance of nurturing wealth ("a successful economy," wrote Gilder, "depends on the proliferation of the rich.") Next was his insistence that individual investment and production are inherently creative, echoing the notion that *supply* (capitalism) creates *demand,* thereby denying a Keynesian role for government:

> Supply creates its own demand. . . . The importance of Says Law[1] is its focus on supply, on the catalytic gifts or investments of capital. It leads economists to concern themselves first with the motives and incentives of individual producers, to return from a preoccupation with

---

1. Say's Law—that supply creates demand—was named for the French economist Jean-Baptiste Say (1767–1832).

distribution and demand and concentrate again on the means of production.

Gilder's third point was the need to curb government ("Since government has become a factor of production, the only way to diminish its impact on prices is to economize on it.") Gilder then hailed the unique and essential role of entrepreneurialism (entrepreneurs "are the heroes of American life"), and finally noted the critical importance of cutting upper-bracket taxes ("To help the poor and middle classes, one must cut the taxes of the rich.")

By the late 1970s inflation had increased tax discontent, and several economic theorists started talking about the central role of tax rates in the rise and fall of nations. Arthur Laffer, and his journalistic Boswell, former *Wall Street Journal* editorial writer Jude Wanniski, played the decisive role—the former with his Laffer Curve, insisting that beyond a certain point increased tax rates reduced rather than raised government revenue, and Wanniski with his book *The Way the World Works*, which publicized Laffer, and then proceeded to describe mankind's rise and fall so as to suggest that tax rates were the key to progress. . . .

The Reagan Boom

The Reagan economic boom was three times longer than the average post-1919 economic recovery. During it 20 million new jobs were created. The mean income of the poorest 20 percent of households rose 5 percent in real terms during the 1980s, and half the people who started the decade in the lowest group had moved up to a higher group by 1990. . . .

Wealth and Poverty predicted the death of socialism. The 1980s were the decade when socialism died and left nothing but a bristling carcass of weapons pointed toward the West. It was the decade when tax rates were cut in 55 nations, following the success of that policy in the US, and

All Income Groups Benefited from the Reagan Boom

The 1980s were a second Gilded Age, in which many Americans made and spent money abundantly. Reagan's eight-year presidency had sparked the creation of 19 million new jobs. So many Americans had been making so much money that the term "millionaire" became meaningless. A Georgia marketing expert, Thomas J. Stanley, counted almost 100,000 "decamillionaires"—people worth over $10 million. Back in 1960 there hadn't been that many plain-vanilla *millionaires*. In 1988, approximately 1.3 million individual Americans were millionaires by assets, up from 574,000 in 1980. . . .

The untold story is how low taxes benefited those Americans who traditionally had not enjoyed the fruits of the country's prosperity. Income levels for almost every demographic group had begun to decline sharply in the late 1970s; but once Reagan's policies took hold, the statistics reversed. Inflation-adjusted median household income for black Americans, for instance, jumped by 16.5 percent between 1982 and 1989, after declining by 10.2 percent between 1978 and 1982.

Esmond Wright, *The American Dream: From Reconstruction to Reagan*. Cambridge, MA: Blackwell, 1996.

revenues dropped in nearly all nations that raised their rates. It was the era when capitalism at last demonstrated conclusively its superiority as an economic system. It was the era when US economic growth rates, long lagging behind the rest of the world, surged ahead of Europe, Africa, and Latin America, and nearly caught up with Japan's for the first time since the early 1950s.

The 1980s also saw the longest peacetime expansion on

record, with the highest rates of investment in capital equipment and the highest sustained rates of manufacturing productivity growth of any postwar recovery. During the 1980s, the US increased its share of global manufacturing output, global exports, and global production. Contrary to thousands of reports to the contrary, US balance sheets mostly improved, with debt as a share of assets dropping drastically for both businesses and households, as equity, net savings, and real estate values rose far more rapidly than indebtedness. Even government debt, as a share of GNP or in relation to real national assets, remained under control by historic and international standards.

After the tax rate reductions urged by *Wealth and Poverty* took effect in 1983 and 1984, total revenues at all levels of government rose some 9 percent a year in real terms, far faster than during the high-tax 1970s. During the 1980s recovery, industrial output rose nearly 40 percent, personal income 20 percent, and all segments of American society benefited from the creation of 22 million new jobs at rising real wages. Black employment rose 30.3 percent and Hispanic employment nearly 50 percent.

Unlike previous decades of growth, moreover, the American expansion of the 1980s came in the face of declining growth in Europe and Japan. Rather than being pulled ahead by faster development abroad, as in previous decades of growth, the US in the 1980s led the world economy. The greatest US triumph was the computer revolution, entirely a product of relentless discipline and entrepreneurial genius in capitalist nations. Computer industry revenues more than quadrupled; unit sales rose by a factor of hundreds; and computer cost-effectiveness rose ten thousand fold. At the end of the decade, US companies still held some two-thirds of the world market, and in critical software and leading-edge microchips their market share was above 70 percent and growing. In particular, the US led in using personal computers, with well over half of the world's 100 million PCs located in the US in 1990. The US still commands three times as much computer power per capita as the Japanese or Europeans. . . .

The Lessons of Reaganomics

By every measure of prosperity, Reaganomics worked. Some 20 million new jobs were created. Inflation was brought under control. And inflation-adjusted income rose for all segments of the population. Much of the credit for this spectacular economic performance goes to the 1981 Economic Recovery Tax Act, which cut tax rates across the board for individuals and reduced the tax burden on business.

If policymakers want to restore economic growth, it seems that they should heed the following lessons of the 1980s:

1. Economic growth is the best weapon against poverty.
2. Economic growth is stimulated by low taxes, particularly low marginal rates.
3. The poor get richer when the rich get richer.
4. If the aim is to make the rich pay more actual taxes, cut their tax rates.
5. Raising taxes on the rich does not help the poor. . . .

Ronald Reagan's legacy is a new epoch of American leadership in liberty and strength. Through his economic policies, Reagan brought the United States to world leadership among major industrial nations in all the key dimensions of economic growth: investment (51 percent growth), industrial production (30 percent growth), manufacturing productivity (26 percent growth), job creation (15 million new jobs), real per-capita income (18 percent increase), and technological innovation (a rising US market share in information technologies).

Defying a worldwide siege of economic stagnation, the Reagan boom was unique in the postwar era. By contrast, the US economic recoveries of the 1950s, 1960s, and 1970s all fed on faster growth abroad. During all these prior up-turns, the US lagged behind Europe and Japan in all the key indices of expansion. During the Reagan era, the US surpassed Europe by a wide margin and caught up with Japan in rates of economic growth, and led the world in growth of investment and employment. Since Reagan assumed office, the US has been the only major industrial nation to increase investment as a share of GNP or to reduce unemployment.

Unlike the last US surge in job creation, in the 1970s, when productivity and real incomes declined, Reagan's world-beating employment boom was accompanied by a record six-year surge in manufacturing-productivity growth, a steady rise in per-capita income, and a striking increase in the quality of jobs.

From the beginning of 1983 through the end of 1989, real economic growth in the United States hit 3.8 percent per year—the Seven Fat Years. By 1990, GNP was 31 percent above 1982 in real, inflation-adjusted terms. Real disposable income *per capita* was 18 percent higher by 1990. The US economy added 18.4 million jobs.

What effect did tax cuts during the period have? Between 1980 and 1990, federal government receipts grew by 99 percent against GNP growth of 102 percent. From the low point in 1983 to the high point in 1989, tax receipts actually grew faster than GNP.

A comparison of purchasing power *per capita* in 1988 showed that the US still has the highest standard of living among developed nations, followed by Canada and Switzerland. West Germany ranked tenth and Japan twelfth.

REAGANOMICS WAS FATALLY FLAWED

ANTHONY S. CAMPAGNA

Ronald Reagan entered office promising to do several things. On the economic front, the Reagan administration vowed to cut taxes, reduce government spending, balance the budget, and reduce inflation. Consistent with Reagan's anticommunism, his administration also planned to increase spending on national defense.

As Anthony S. Campagna points out in the following selection from his book *The Economy in the Reagan Years*, some of these goals were contradictory. For example, Reagan did manage to cut taxes shortly after taking office in 1981. According to supply-side economic theory, writes Campagna, cutting taxes was somehow supposed to increase, rather than decrease, tax revenue. But, maintains the author, supply-side economics was a baseless theory, an illusion created to support the conservative agenda. In reality, defense spending increased while tax revenues did not, and the national deficit soared. Campagna, a professor of economics at the University of Vermont, maintains that Reagan had no real plan for delivering on all his various promises, and that he instead simply told voters what they wanted to hear.

M R. REAGAN TOLD THE NATION WHAT IT WANTED TO HEAR. His message was upbeat and optimistic just as he himself had always been; it was not a phony stance nor was it perceived as such. The public wanted hope, the restoration of pride of country, and it wanted to dream. Reagan was determined to provide them and set out on a course designed to harvest these underlying and often unspoken yearnings. . . .

Of course, people also took whatever part of his program that appealed to them and dismissed the rest as irrelevant. How can I benefit, not what is good for the country, became the rallying cry around the affable Reagan, ushering in the era of greed as a national virtue. Those who stood to gain from his program naturally backed him, often without regard for the effects of the total agenda. This will become more evident and discernible when the program is described below. . . .

The Reagan Agenda

In the speeches he made during his transformation from a liberal Democrat to a conservative Republican, largely as an after-dinner speaker growing out of his tenure on a television show sponsored by General Electric, and throughout his campaigns for the presidency, Reagan kept harping on three themes: taxes should be cut, government spending and involvement in private affairs should be reduced, and national defense spending should be increased to ensure that the United States was strong enough to meet any challenge. He was ever faithful to these beliefs, right up to the time he left office. He would not be budged from these positions no matter how eloquent the arguments made to the contrary.

This then is basically the Reagan agenda, and although others added elements to it that came to be known as Reaganomics, he would remain loyal only to the three basic themes. This was characteristic of Reagan who resisted all attempts to move him away from his basic biases, leaving much of the remainder of the agenda to others. He had no grand designs, no conception of how best to achieve these ends, and no interest in many of the programs that were initiated in his name. He knew what he wanted to achieve and delegated much of everything else to his aides. His was not an analytical mind, and he did not think in the abstract. His management style was called passive, detached, and disinterested, and although many, inside and outside government, questioned his intellectual ability, he demonstrated a faculty to stick with what interested him and leave the rest to others. His knowledge of economics was minimal, and complicated arguments of any kind went beyond him. He simply was unprepared for the job and did not wish to engage in the type of study that would have remedied the matter. Still, he was unwavering in his desire to achieve his lifelong goals, and when these goals were not achieved or were compromised, he refused to acknowledge error or defeat.

During the campaign, Reagan kept hammering away on his favorite themes, punctuated by anecdotes about welfare cheats and the costs of government regulations. After the election, the campaign pledges, promises, and the usual political rhetoric were finally codified in the presidential message to Congress issued on February 18, 1981 called *A Program for Economic Recovery*. The plan for economic recovery included four parts: the reduction in the growth of federal spending but an *increase* in national defense spending; the reduction in tax rates; the reduction in government regulations; and a monetary policy consistent with the other elements of the program. Three of these components were the themes emphasized by Reagan, and the fourth was added to complete the plan. A closer look at each part, however, reveals other subsidiary goals as well and should have alerted everyone to the inherent contradictions in the overall plan.

The Allure of Tax Reduction

First, the reduction in government expenditures during the campaign were only supposed to eliminate waste in government spending. Who could be opposed to that? After the election, the cuts in government spending went far beyond cutting out waste to slashing spending on a wide variety of social programs. Only the "truly needy" (the poor, elderly, unemployed, veterans) would be protected and supported by government. All other entitlement programs, subsidy programs, and public sector investment programs, were up for review, as were the number of government personnel and federal grants to states and localities. These reductions in the growth of federal expenditures were to lead to a *balanced budget* by 1984 (1983 during the campaign) and a surplus by 1985.

The reduction in federal income tax rates was supposed to provide the necessary incentive for economic agents to begin to invest and produce more. Greater investment would provide more jobs, increase labor productivity, encourage economic growth, and, in the end, the greater economic activity would bring in more tax revenue, some said enough to cover the revenue loss of the tax rate reduction. If the tax reductions did not cause an increase in the federal deficit, there was no need to worry about cuts in government spending if that should prove a problem. If taxes could be cut without worrying about increasing the budget deficit, and without worrying about government spending, what politician could resist this siren's song?

Supply-Side Economics: A Matter of Faith

This was the same song sung by [industrialist, financier, and former secretary of the treasury] Andrew Mellon in the 1920s when he fought to reduce taxes for the same reason—high taxes discourage productive use of resources. This precedent for supply-side economics was not empirically based then and, when reinvented by Arthur Laffer, was not empirically based then either. Laffer, as did Mellon, persuaded a small but vocal group that tax revenues vary with the tax rate! Using a parabolic (bell-shaped) curve, he was able to demonstrate that tax revenues rise with the tax rates until some optimal rate was reached; thereafter, as tax rates rose, revenues fell. It follows that tax rates beyond the optimal one were undesirable for they hinder productive investment without bringing in more revenue. It also follows that a reduction in tax rates would *increase* revenues if the tax rate were beyond the optimal one. So far, this Laffer curve was nothing but a tautology and added nothing to our knowledge. Supply-siders, however, were convinced, without the benefit of empirical analysis, that tax rates in the United States were beyond the optimal ones and that reductions in tax rates would stimulate productive activity and increase tax revenues.

Many economists would have favored tax reductions for a variety of reasons, but few would have professed to know anything about optimal tax rates, or would have been willing to predict what would occur to productive effort if rates were cut. To supply-side economists, such reservations were the result of past faulty thinking, and supply-side predictions became a matter of dogma—of faith. So the Kemp-Roth tax bill of reducing tax rates by 30% became part of the Reagan agenda; it fit into his pattern of thinking and verified his own experience of high taxes and reduced effort when he was in Hollywood. High tax rates discouraged making more than four pictures a year back in World War II.

Deregulation

The relaxation of government regulations was designed to reduce the costs of compliance by industry and reduce the administrative costs of the bureaucracy created by them. Get the government off our backs was the campaign cry, and let industry compete. U.S. industry must not be shackled if it was to meet the growing competitive threat from abroad. Moreover, burdensome regulations affected economic growth because they discouraged research and development, reduced investment, raised labor costs, and reduced competition. Again, no evidence was supplied to support these contentions.

Monetary policy was to be the restraining force to bring down inflation. By restricting the rate of growth of the money supply, the economy should be able to expand without inflation. In the long run it was predicted that interest rates would come down as well.

Finally, one element of the plan that is frequently un-

The Myth of a Conservative Reagan Revolution

When Ronald Reagan entered office in 1981, many liberals worried that the "Reagan Revolution" would entail the abolition of federal social programs such as Social Security, Medicare, and welfare. Yet when the president left office in 1989, many conservatives lamented that Reagan had failed to substantially cut government spending. The following passage, excerpted from an essay by John Robson of the Fraser Institute, typifies this point of view.

Despite a lot of rhetoric both from the administration and from its critics, domestic spending under Reagan went up; the share of Gross National Product (GNP) taken by the federal government went up; the deficit went up; entitlements expanded. Regulation decreased somewhat; but, for the most part, the growth of the welfare state proceeded as though Jimmy Carter were still in office. And on a more minor but important issue, when Reagan came into office, one-eighth of U.S. imports were subject to restraints, often with the insincere label "voluntary"; by the time he left, the figure was more like one-fourth. Readers may be surprised to hear this with respect to economic and social policy, because

deremphasized was the change in expectations that the whole program was supposed to bring. In *A Program for Economic Recovery*, the importance of this feature is clearly stated:

> The ultimate importance of this program for sustained economic growth will arise not only from the positive effects of the individual components, important as they are. Rather, it will be the dramatic improvement in the

commentators generally described and condemned the wholesale dismantling of the welfare state under Reagan even though this was not happening; a typical cartoon showed George Bush saying "Read my lips" and a kid replying "I can't, you guys cut funding for education"— which is very funny, except that federal education funding went up substantially, not down, under Reagan. . . .

In reality, Reagan's presidency represented a rhetorical vacillation between smaller government and better government, with a policy emphasis on the latter. He failed to disentangle the state from the economy as he had intended. He faced many political obstacles along the way, but the absence of a legacy is more the product of lack of resolve and conviction than it is of political difficulties. In the broader sense he did not reverse a nation in decline. Despite the alarmed rhetoric of modern liberals, he did not bring conservatism to Washington even temporarily. He talked like a conservative, governed like a neoconservative, and left liberalism in America as strong as or stronger than it had been in 1981.

John Robson, "The Reagan Revolution: Interpretive Essay," in John E. Findling and Frank W. Thackeray, eds., *Events That Changed America in the Twenty-First Century*. Westport, CT: Greenwood Press, 1996.

underlying economic environment and outlook that will set a new and more positive direction to economic decisions throughout the economy.

Prospects for the Plan

Omitting the details, this is the outline of the plan for economic recovery. Most economists, even those sympathetic to the aims of the administration, would have some difficulty believing in a proposal that promised to cut taxes, balance the budget, increase spending on national defense, reduce inflation, cut government spending, and change expectations simultaneously! Clearly, elements of the plan were contradictory and mutually exclusive. Pursuing an expansionary fiscal policy and a contractionary monetary policy is alone sufficient cause for skepticism. How could such a program be taken seriously?

During the campaign, George Bush, a rival presidential candidate, labeled it "voodoo economics." There were internal conflicts as well, as traditional Republicans battled the new comers—the supply-siders. Consider that the administration brought to Washington three (and probably more) groups who were bound to disagree. The supply-siders wanted a tax cut for economic stimulation; the monetarists wanted tight money to fight inflation; and the budget balancers wanted to eliminate the deficit and balance the budget annually. If the tax cuts were passed, would not the expansion be limited by high interest rates caused by tight money? If the tax cuts were passed without significant reductions in government expenditures, would that not increase the deficit? Should not government expenditures be reduced before taxes are cut, as conservatives had maintained since [republican leader and 1964 presidential candidate Barry] Goldwater expressed their aims? These debates raged within the administration and in Congress as soon as the groups began to press their views.

Where was Reagan in all this? According to Cannon,

. . . [Reagan] was far more interested in economic recovery than he was concerned about the deficits that would be the by-products of his policies. The quarrel between supply-siders and traditionalists completely bored him. Reagan wanted both tax cuts and spending reductions. He believed that he would get more of each if he did not choose between the competing policies.

This is typical Reagan who always found it difficult to choose sides when his aides differed, and either asked them to find a compromise or split the difference (often resulting in ludicrous policies) or failed to offer any direction giving his aides control over policy or leaving them confused as to the direction the president wanted to take.

Of all Reagan's advisors, perhaps the one most familiar with the entire economic program was David Stockman, the head of the Office of Management and Budget (OMB). To Stockman was given the task of translating the overall plan into numbers. He also found that "The broad policy architecture of the plan was riddled with potential contradictions." Stockman really mastered the budget numbers and became the administration's authority on the economic plan. Later, he was to admit that

None of us really understands what's going on with all these numbers . . . the defense numbers got out of control and we were doing the whole budget-cutting exercise so frenetically . . . And it didn't quite mesh . . . Kemp-Roth [the bill that was eventually modified to become the Economic Recovery Tax Act of 1981] was always a Trojan Horse to bring down the top rate . . . Supply-side is "trickle-down-theory."

A Plan Built on Deception, Illusion, and Hope

Without belaboring the point, it is clear that there were contradictions in the program, that they were recognized by those in charge of the policy, and that nothing was done to amend the basic thrust of the economic plan. On a more technical level, it was pointed out to the administration that the monetary policy was inconsistent with the economic growth forecasted. The growth in the nominal GNP for 1981 was predicted to be about 11%, with the rise in the Consumer Price Index (CPI) predicted at about 11%. However, the rate of growth in the money supply was to be about 5%. How, then, could the economic growth be financed? Unless the velocity of money increased phenomenally, not very likely unless interest rates *fell* or spending patterns changed dramatically, there would not be sufficient means to finance the expansion. The administration simply refused to deal with this glaring contradiction, less it upset the alleged favorable expectations that were being created.

So at the start of the alleged economic revolution, we have a president with a few long-held biases against taxes and government spending and a conviction that America was weak militarily. We are told that he had no grand designs for how best to achieve these vague desires nor what the effects on the country would be if they were enacted. He did not think in the abstract and was continually surprised to learn of possible adverse effects of proposals being made in his name. Biases cannot substitute for objective analysis and detachment cannot substitute for leadership. Therefore, when the policies did not seem coherent and the numbers did not add up, those around him, his loyal advisors, had to contend with a president who did not care to contemplate options or revise his thinking; hence, they did not tell him of the problems! They had to proceed with plans that were contradictory, turning aside all criticisms with a fallback position that amounted to religious dogma. And in the case of a major architect of the economic plan, David Stockman, even that was not sufficient once he lost the faith and resorted to deception to please his superiors.

So the economic plan was built on deception, on illusion, on hope, and on biases. These are hardly the foundations for a genuine revolution. Yet, Ronald Reagan was probably the only kind of president able to carry it off. A leader who knew what he wanted and who would not be deterred from it sent the right signals to everyone in the administration; a leader who did not know very much about the details of how to get what he wanted but who knew enough to surround himself with loyal aides who did certainly warrants some claim to being an effective, if accidental, strategist.

Reagan was aided in this by a desperate public willing to risk stability for change, in aides who were willing to protect the president from challenges to his knowledge and biases, and in Congress which was willing to be led into policies it frequently was suspicious of but was afraid of the popular president.

Reagan's Economic Policies Favored the Rich

Howard Zinn

Ronald Reagan wanted to reduce the size of the federal government, and in practice this often meant eliminating or reducing the budget for social programs such as welfare and school lunches. Reagan also favored cutting taxes for all income groups, in contrast to the liberal idea of progressive taxation, which holds that individuals at very high income levels should pay more in taxes than those in lower income brackets.

Reagan's agenda remains highly controversial. While his supporters point to the 1980s as a decade of prosperity, Reagan's critics charge that the main legacy of Reaganomics is increased income inequality. In the following excerpt from his book *A People's History of the United States*, Howard Zinn maintains that Reagan's economic policies were designed to benefit mainly the very rich. Zinn argues that Reagan's cuts in social spending adversely affected millions of Americans trying to survive in poverty, while the Reagan tax cuts benefited the very wealthy more than they did the middle or working classes. Zinn is a professor of political science at Boston University.

———

THE PRESERVATION OF A HUGE MILITARY ESTABLISHMENT and the retention of profit levels of oil corporations appeared to be twin objectives of the Reagan-Bush administrations. Shortly after Ronald Reagan took office, twenty-

Excerpted from *A People's History of the United States*, by Howard Zinn. Copyright ©1980 by Howard Zinn. Reprinted by permission of HarperCollins Publishers, Inc.

three oil industry executives contributed $270,000 to re-decorate the White House living quarters. According to the Associated Press:

> The solicitation drive . . . came four weeks after the President decontrolled oil prices, a decision worth $2 billion to the oil industry . . . Jack Hodges of Oklahoma City, owner of Core Oil and Gas Company, said: "The top man of this country ought to live in one of the top places. Mr. Reagan has helped the energy business."

While he built up the military (allocations of over a trillion dollars in his first four years in office), Reagan tried to pay for this with cuts in benefits for the poor. There would be $140 billion of cuts in social programs through 1984 and an increase of $181 billion for "defense" in the same period. He also proposed tax cuts of $190 billion (most of this going to the wealthy).

Despite the tax cuts and the military appropriations, Reagan insisted he would still balance the budget because the tax cuts would so stimulate the economy as to generate new revenue. Nobel Prize–winning economist Wassily Leontief remarked dryly: "This is not likely to happen. In fact, I personally guarantee that it will not happen."

Indeed, Department of Commerce figures showed that periods of lowered corporate taxes (1973–1975, 1979–1982) did not at all show higher capital investment, but a steep drop. The sharpest rise of capital investment (1975–1979) took place when corporate taxes were slightly higher than they had been the preceding five years.

The Human Consequences of Budget Cuts

The human consequences of Reagan's budget cuts went deep. For instance, Social Security disability benefits were terminated for 350,000 people. A man injured in an oil field accident was forced to go back to work, the federal government overruling both the company doctor and a state supervisor who testified that he was too disabled to work. The man died, and federal officials said, "We have a P.R. problem." A war hero of Vietnam, Roy Benavidez, who had been presented with the Congressional Medal of Honor by Reagan, was told by Social Security officials that the shrapnel pieces in his heart, arms, and leg did not prevent him from working. Appearing before a Congressional committee, he denounced Reagan.

Unemployment grew in the Reagan years. In the year 1982, 30 million people were unemployed all or part of the year. One result was that over 16 million Americans lost medical insurance, which was often tied to holding a job. In Michigan, where the unemployment rate was the highest in the country, the infant death rate began to rise in 1981.

New requirements eliminated free school lunches for more than one million poor children, who depended on the meal for as much as half of their daily nutrition. Millions of children entered the ranks of the officially declared "poor" and soon a quarter of the nation's children—twelve million—were living in poverty. In parts of Detroit, one-third of the children were dying before their first birthday, and the *New York Times* commented: "Given what's happening to the hungry in America, this Administration has cause only for shame."

Reagan's Attack on Welfare

Welfare became an object of attack: aid to single mothers with children through the AFDC (Aid to Families with Dependent Children) program, food stamps, health care for the poor through Medicaid. For most people on welfare (the benefits differed from state to state) this meant $500 to $700 a month in aid, leaving them well below the poverty level of about $900 a month. Black children were four times as likely as white children to grow up on welfare.

Early in the Reagan administration, responding to the argument that government aid was not needed, that private enterprise would take care of poverty, a mother wrote to her local newspaper:

> I am on Aid to Families with Dependent Children, and both my children are in school. . . . I have graduated from college with distinction, 128th in a class of over 1000, with a B.A. in English and sociology. I have experience in library work, child care, social work and counseling.

> I have been to the CETA office. They have nothing for me. . . . I also go every week to the library to scour the newspaper Help Wanted ads. I have kept a copy of every cover letter that I have sent out with my resume; the stack is inches thick. I have applied for jobs paying as little as $8000 a year. I work part-time in a library for $3.50 an hour; welfare reduces my allotment to compensate. . . .

> It appears we have employment offices that can't employ, governments that can't govern and an economic system that can't produce jobs for people ready to work. . . .

> Last week I sold my bed to pay for the insurance on my car, which, in the absence of mass transportation, I need to go job hunting. I sleep on a piece of rubber foam somebody gave me.

> So this is the great American dream my parents came to this country for: Work hard, get a good education, follow the rules, and you will be rich. I don't want to be rich. I just want to be able to feed my children and live with some semblance of dignity. . . .

Democrats often joined Republicans in denouncing welfare programs. Presumably, this was done to gain political support from a middle-class public that believed they were paying taxes to support teenage mothers and people they thought too lazy to work. Much of the public did not know, and were not informed by either political leaders or

The Failure of Reaganomics

Ultimately, Reaganomics was a failure. It produced big political dividends for the Republicans, and it may have contributed to rapid economic growth during the 1980s. But it was, at its core, a governing philosophy based on a deeply flawed economic notion: that tax cuts, especially large tax cuts for the rich, would not worsen the government's budget deficit. . . .

Reaganomics simply didn't do what Ronald Reagan promised when he swept into power in 1981. And in the end, both Reagan and Bush were repeatedly forced to ratchet Reaganomics back in the face of its frightening effects on the nation's level of indebtedness. . . .

The statistics are staggering: Since Ronald Reagan first took office, the budget deficit has more than tripled, from $79 billion in 1981 and $290 billion [in 1992], while total government debt held by the public has soared from less than $800 billion to more than $3 trillion.

The nation has been mortgaged. In 1981, government debt equaled 25% of gross domestic product, the nation's total output of goods and services; [in 1992] it is more than half. Now, 3.5% of GDP, roughly $200 billion, goes just to pay the annual interest on the federal debt.

The bottom line is that the most profligate government spending of all time came during an extended period of conservative Republican rule.

James Risen, "History May Judge Reaganomics Very Harshly," *Los Angeles Times*, November 8, 1992.

the media, that welfare took a tiny part of the taxes, and military spending took a huge chunk of it. Yet, the public's attitude on welfare was different from that of the two major parties. It seemed that the constant attacks on welfare by politicians, reported endlessly in the press and on television, did not succeed in eradicating a fundamental generosity felt by most Americans.

A *New York Times*/CBS News poll conducted in early 1992 showed that public opinion on welfare changed depending on how the question was worded. If the word "welfare" was used, 44 percent of those questioned said too much was being spent on welfare (while 50 percent said either that the right amount was being spent, or that too little was being spent). But when the question was about "assistance to the poor," only 13 percent thought too much was being spent, and 64 percent thought too little was being spent.

This suggested that both parties were trying to manufacture an antihuman-needs mood by constant derogatory use of the word "welfare," and then to claim they were acting in response to public opinion. The Democrats as well as the Republicans had strong connections to wealthy corporations. Kevin Phillips, a Republican analyst of national politics, wrote in 1990 that the Democratic Party was "history's second-most enthusiastic capitalist party."

Catering to the Superrich

Phillips pointed out that the greatest beneficiaries of government policy during the Republican presidencies of Ronald Reagan and George Bush were the superrich: "It was the truly wealthy, more than anyone else, who flourished under Reagan. . . . The 1980s were the triumph of upper America . . . the political ascendancy of the rich, and a glorification of capitalism, free markets, and finance."

When government policy enriched the already rich, it was not called welfare. This was not as obvious as the monthly checks to the poor; it most often took the form of generous changes in the tax system.

In *America: Who Really Pays The Taxes?*, two investigative reporters with the *Philadelphia Inquirer*, Donald Barlett and James Steele, traced the path by which tax rates for the very rich got lower and lower. It was not the Republicans but the Democrats—the Kennedy-Johnson administrations—who, under the guise of "tax reform," first lowered the World War II–era rate of 91 percent on incomes over $400,000 a year to 70 percent. During the Carter administration (though over his objections) Democrats and Republicans in Congress joined to give even more tax breaks to the rich.

The Reagan administration, with the help of Democrats in Congress, lowered the tax rate on the very rich to 50 percent and in 1986 a coalition of Republicans and Democrats sponsored another "tax reform" bill that lowered the top rate to 28 percent. Barlett and Steele noted that a schoolteacher, a factory worker, and a billionaire could all pay 28 percent. The idea of a "progressive" income in which the rich paid at higher rates than everyone else was now almost dead. . . .

By the end of the Reagan years, the gap between rich and poor in the United States had grown dramatically. Where in 1980, the chief executive officers (CEOs) of corporations made forty times as much in salary as the average factory worker, by 1989 they were making ninety-three times as much. In the dozen years from 1977 to 1989, the before-tax income of the richest 1 percent rose 77 percent; meanwhile, for the poorest two-fifths of the population, there was no gain at all, indeed a small decline.

And because of favorable changes for the rich in the tax structure, the richest 1 percent, in the decade ending in 1990, saw their after-tax income increase 87 percent. In the same period, the after-tax income of the lower four-fifths of the population either went down 5 percent (at the poorest level) or went up no more than 8.6 percent.

PRESIDENTS
and their
DECISIONS

CHAPTER
2

THE END OF
THE COLD WAR

Renewing the Cold War

Andrew E. Busch and Elizabeth Edwards Spalding

U.S.–Soviet relations in the first few years of Reagan's presidency were characterized by increased hostility between the two rival nations. Reagan himself held very strong anticommunist views, and his administration's foreign policies matched his anti-Soviet rhetoric. Reagan was committed to the deployment of nuclear missiles in Europe and to winning the arms race as a whole. Under what became known as the Reagan Doctrine, the United States began to openly aid anticommunist forces in Third World nations such as Nicaragua and El Salvador. All this was in sharp contrast to the 1970s policy of détente, under which the United States and the Soviet Union had sought to reduce tensions and slow the arms race.

In the following selection, Andrew E. Busch, a professor of political science at the University of Denver, and Elizabeth Edwards Spalding, a professor of government and foreign affairs at the University of Virginia, maintain that Reagan's stepping-up of Cold War hostilities in his first years in office marked the beginning of the end of that conflict. Writing 10 years after Reagan's 1983 denunciation of the Soviet Union as an "evil empire," they contend that other key decisions of that year—such as the announcement of the Strategic Defense Initiative (SDI) and the invasion of Grenada—were the crucial first parts of Reagan's broad strategy to gain an upper hand in the Cold War.

Excerpted from Andrew E. Busch and Elizabeth Edwards Spalding, "1983: Awakening from Orwell's Nightmare," *Policy Review*, Fall 1993. Reprinted by permission of *Policy Review*.

THIS YEAR MARKS THE 10TH ANNIVERSARY OF THE BEGIN-ning of the end of the Cold War. Although it was difficult to foresee at the time, a series of events in 1983 would come together to stop the seemingly inexorable advance of Soviet totalitarianism and to lay the groundwork for the eventual triumph of the West.

These events were neither inevitable nor self-executing. They depended upon the decisions of men, and of one man in particular—Ronald Reagan—who understood the meaning of this century, the nature of the Cold War, and the set of circumstances that he and his country faced. In 1983, the elements of President Reagan's strategy joined for the first time, making possible the successes that wrought the changes in Eastern Europe in 1989 and culminated in the 1991 implosion of the Soviet regime and the rest of its empire.

The Evil Empire Speech

The central theme of President Reagan's foreign policy was the ethical distinction he continually made between the West and the Soviet bloc. At his first press conference as president, Mr. Reagan bluntly referred to the nature of Leninist "morality," correctly telling a contemptuous press corps that Soviet leaders "reserve unto themselves the right to commit any crime, to lie, to cheat," in order to achieve their objective of world communism. In a famous speech before the British Parliament in June 1982, the president called for a "crusade for freedom," and he predicted that it would be communism, not freedom, that would end up on the "ash-heap of history."

But President Reagan's most important Cold War speech was his March 1983 address to religious broadcasters in which he called the Soviet Union an "evil empire":

Let us be aware that while they [the Soviet regime] preach the supremacy of the state, declare its omnipotence over individual man, and predict its eventual domination over all people on the earth, they are the focus of evil in the modern world. . . . I urge you to beware the temptation of pride—the temptation of blithely declaring yourselves above it all and labelling both sides equally at fault, to ignore the facts of history and the aggressive impulses of an evil empire, to simply call the arms race a giant misunderstanding and thereby remove yourself from the struggle between right and wrong and good and evil.

Mr. Reagan underscored the message that no longer would the United States remain silent about the true nature of the Soviet regime. Apprehending the importance of ideas and the danger of truth far better than Mr. Reagan's critics did, the Kremlin construed the evil empire speech as an act of political aggression.

Many people understood from the beginning that Mr. Reagan was right. What since has become clear, however, is the effect that his pronouncement had on those who lived in that empire. Among others, Lech Walesa later maintained that the evil empire speech was an epochal event in the long struggle of Eastern Europe to be free; even former Soviet officials since have acknowledged that the speech, in the words of Reagan biographer Edmund Morris, helped "the motherland realize . . . it was indeed evil." President Reagan's ultimate vindication came when the foreign minister of the Russian Federation, Andrei Kozyrev, added his concurrence: The Soviet Union, Mr. Kozyrev said in 1992, had been an "evil empire."

The legitimacy of this rhetorical counteroffensive was reinforced in September 1983 when the Soviets under Yuri Andropov shot down a Korean Airlines passenger jet, KAL 007, demonstrating with appalling clarity the accuracy of President Reagan's March charge. The incident not only gave momentum to Mr. Reagan's exposure of the nature of the Soviet regime; it also shut down a nascent movement within the administration for a more accommodationist stance toward the Kremlin.

The year 1983 also was significant for the intermediate-range nuclear forces (INF) deployments in Western Europe. In November 1981, President Reagan reaffirmed the 1979 North Atlantic Treaty Organization (NATO) dual-track decision, then championed by West German Chancellor Helmut Schmidt, to deploy missiles and to negotiate for arms control. With the Soviets more aggressive than ever as they deployed one SS-20 a week, President Reagan sought to strengthen the West through the deployment of 108 Pershing II and 464 ground-launched cruise missiles, scheduled to begin in November 1983. To do so, he had to overcome one of the most powerful Soviet propaganda offensives in the entire Cold War.

Peace Movements

As the Soviets had attempted to stymie NATO's founding and the Western alliance in the late 1940s through subversion, aggression, and totalitarian propaganda, so too, they tried to shape a situation favorable to Kremlin hegemony in the superpower nuclear age. It was all part of the same Cold War. The key to success, the Kremlin knew, lay in dividing and sapping NATO of its unity and meaning. The Soviets hoped, at a minimum, that opposition to the Pershings and cruise missiles would become a substantial lever to crack the Atlantic alliance. To this end, they sponsored and inspired large portions of the nuclear freeze movement in Europe. . . .

Euromissile deployment proceeded on schedule, and, more important, the Atlantic alliance held strong. Late 1983 into 1984 was a period of NATO cohesion unprecedented since the collective defense organization's founding. NATO allies saw through the Kremlin tactics aimed at straining Western unity in November 1983, when the Soviets walked out of the START talks in Geneva. The allies concurred with President Reagan that negotiations could come only after the establishment of Western strength and acknowledgment of that strength by the Soviet Union. As Mrs. Thatcher noted that Reagan "strengthened not only America's defenses, but also the will of America's allies."

The SDI Wild Card

President Reagan's revolution in strategic defense also came in 1983. His March 23 speech challenged the very nature of modern warfare. It dazed the Soviets and helped to break the back of the nuclear freeze movement. Mr. Reagan rejected the logic of mutually assured destruction (MAD) and flexible response, which left civilian populations totally vulnerable to nuclear destruction. He announced the goal of making nuclear weapons "impotent and obsolete." As the president said, "What if free people could live secure in the knowledge that their security did not rest upon the threat of instant U.S. retaliation to deter a Soviet attack, that we could intercept and destroy strategic ballistic missiles before they reached our own soil or that of our allies?"

With this March 1983 speech, President Reagan finished putting forth his vision to transform radically the global strategic situation and the nature of defense. Mr. Reagan showed that the West had the political courage and know-how to fight and win what Soviet thinkers commonly called the scientific-technical revolution in military affairs. The Kremlin referred over and over to American militarization of space. Soviet leaders Konstantin Chernenko and especially Mikhail Gorbachev attempted vigorously to derail SDI. Mr. Gorbachev and his Foreign Ministers Eduard Shevardnadze and Aleksandr Bessmertnykh now have conceded the importance of SDI in driving change in the Soviet Union in the late 1980s. President Reagan had begun to move the West beyond containment with the promise of propelling the world beyond communism and Cold War.

Turning the Tide in El Salvador

As Ronald Reagan pursued a two-track strategy in Europe and on defense policy—one track securing the base of the Western alliance and restoring our deterrent capacity, the other track seizing the initiative with SDI—he also constructed a two-tiered policy in the Third World. First, President Reagan sought to brace American friends and prevent further Soviet penetration. Second, he began to pursue the offensive against many of the Kremlin clients that had taken power in the 1970s: Cambodia, Angola, Ethiopia, Afghanistan, Grenada, and Nicaragua. No other year was as pivotal to the president's strategy as was 1983.

It is easy to forget that, throughout 1982 and 1983, a serious question existed as to whether the United States would be able to ensure the survival of a fledgling democracy in El Salvador. When the communists launched a major offensive in late 1983 that scored several important victories, the Faribundo Marti National Liberation Front (FMLN) was at its peak, leading *Newsweek* to hypothesize that the Salvadoran army might collapse before Christmas. There can be little doubt that failure in El Salvador would have worsened prospects for democracy in Guatemala and Honduras, if not prompted their fall. In that event, Mexico would have been the next likely target. . . .

Although the issue had surfaced in 1982, vigorous debate over aid to the Nicaraguan resistance exploded in the summer of 1983. The aid battle and the Contras' fortunes see-sawed throughout the 1980s, but 1983 was the first year the United States concentrated significant political attention on the Nicaraguan resistance. It was in 1983 that the Reagan administration, for the first time, frankly made the case for aid. Turning back attempts in Congress to end existing funding for the Contras, the administration also proposed expanding Contra troop strength to 15,000. The Nicaraguan resistance already had reached 12,000 men under arms, higher than any other guerrilla army in Latin America, and the Contras grew bolder.

The Reagan Doctrine Defined

A turning point had been reached in policy toward Nicaragua and, more generally, in policy toward Soviet Third-World clients: "covert" aid to resistance forces increasingly would be covert in name only. While the successes in El Salvador were crucial, they came within the

The Man Who Won the Cold War

Edwin Meese III was a counselor to President Reagan from 1981 to 1985, and attorney general from 1985 to 1988. In the following excerpt, adapted from his book With Reagan: The Inside Story, *Meese contends that Ronald Reagan is given too little credit for his key role in ending the Cold War.*

From a post–Cold War perspective, the main principles of the Reagan program may seem self-evident. Viewing the rubble of the Berlin Wall, the upheavals that have transformed Eastern Europe, and the internal collapse of the soviet regime, hardly anyone can doubt that Communism was indeed an "Evil Empire" and a failed economic system. Such points have been affirmed by the former leaders of the Communist world itself.

Yet at the time Reagan was making these statements and pursuing these policies there was nothing self-evident about them. On the contrary, he was roundly attacked both for his general analysis of the situation, and for nearly all the specific steps he took in carrying out his policy—the defense buildup, INF deployments,

framework of traditional containment policy. At the same time, a much more proactive policy in the Third World began to take shape in Nicaragua—what became known as the Reagan Doctrine. The Reagan administration had staked out a position putting the U.S. on the side of anti-communist forces not only materially but also morally, and it had given notice to the Soviets that the Brezhnev Doctrine was not an acceptable point of departure for superpower relations. In addition, aid to the Nicaraguan resistance was linked with aid to El Salvador as two sides—offensive and defensive—of a coherent policy. . . .

aid to anti-Communist resistance forces, curtailment of technology transfer, SDI.

Even in the aftermath of the Communist collapse Reagan critics were reluctant to credit President Reagan with the accuracy of his vision or the correctness of his policy. Many discussions of the Communist debacle completely ignore the impact of the Reagan strategy, attributing the demise of the "Evil Empire" to a change of heart on the part of the Communists, or to unnamed forces that somehow brought about the toppling of the system. . . .

Former British Prime Minister Margaret Thatcher knew Gorbachev and Reagan well. She said Gorbachev was a man we could do business with, but she didn't credit him with the collapse of Communism. That honor was due to Ronald Reagan, whose foreign policy accomplishments she summed up at a 1991 Heritage Foundation dinner in Washington: "He won the Cold War without firing a shot."

Edwin Meese III, "The Man Who Won the Cold War," *Policy Review*, Summer 1992.

Grenada: Puncturing Brezhnev

The most dramatic and abrupt reversal of the Soviet design throughout the eight years of the Reagan presidency came on October 25, 1983, when U.S. airborne troops and Marines landed on the island of Grenada. This small island country 100 miles off the coast of Venezuela had fallen into the Soviet orbit in March 1979, after Maurice Bishop, a Marxist lawyer, and his "New Jewel Movement" seized power in a *coup d'état.* For the next four-and-a-half years, Grenada moved closer to serving as a base for Kremlin ambitions and power projection in the Caribbean, a threat that President Reagan had identified and warned of in his March SDI speech.

When Mr. Bishop was overthrown and executed in mid-October by even more hard-line communist elements of the New Jewel Movement, Grenada's small island neighbors, in the form of the Organization of East Caribbean States, invited U.S. intervention. President Reagan ordered the invasion to proceed on October 25. When the operation ended a few days later, 75 percent of the American people and 90 percent of the Grenadian people polled had supported the action.

The American invasion of Grenada was the first major use of force by the United States since the Vietnam War, and it was the first time that U.S. troops had been used to liberate a communist country. Vast stockpiles of Soviet weapons and a collection of damning documents were discovered, American students were evacuated successfully, Cuban forces were defeated in battle, and the Brezhnev Doctrine was punctured. For the first time in recent memory, the United States was on the offensive for freedom, both substantively and directly.

Grenada was a tiny island with a tiny population of 85,000, but its significance was huge. Historians should record that October 24, 1983, represented the high-water mark of the Soviet empire. Never again would the communists in the Kremlin control as much territory or wield as much influence as they did on the day before Army Rangers landed at Point Salines. At the end of 1983, the Soviet Third-World strategy was thwarted in key respects, and important American allies had been reinvigorated.

Shock Waves of the Economic Rebound

Finally, victory against the Soviet Union in the Cold War was undergirded by the remarkable recovery of the U.S. economy from the stagflation of the late 1970s and early 1980s. In January 1983, the United States began a 93-month period of sustained, noninflationary economic growth. By the time the expansion ended in the summer of 1990 during the Bush administration, the Berlin Wall no longer existed.

This economic expansion had three important effects. First, it ensured the 1984 re-election of Ronald Reagan and the continuation of the policies that were instrumental to victory in the primary theater of the Cold War. Second, it guaranteed the economic resources necessary to pursue these policies and, more generally, to maintain a strong American presence in the world. Lastly, the ability of the United States to pull itself out of its economic doldrums had a momentous impact on the Soviets' faith in their Marxist beliefs. America's economic growth disproved the "inevitability" of the collapse of capitalism, which the Soviets had thought to be at hand. Indeed, the recovery led to a serious re-appraisal of economic collectivism throughout the West and the Third World, inducing many socialist governments to introduce capitalist reforms.

The Vulnerable Empire

Ronald Reagan entered office determined to turn around the Cold War and complete the policy of containment. In both theory and practice, President Reagan grasped that the Soviet Union was at a crisis point in the early 1980s, and he saw clearly the central contradiction within Kremlin policy that made the Soviet empire vulnerable: it was bankrupt economically, yet was engaging in renewed heights of external aggression. By 1980, still on a perpetual wartime footing because of their ideology, the Soviets invested more than two to three times what the United States did on military spending. Mr. Reagan aimed to push this Soviet paradox of internal decay and outward expansion, all the while reminding the world of the tyrannical nature of the Soviet regime. In this task he succeeded. Although their economy continued to falter and their military spending consumed over 25 percent of GNP by 1987, the Soviets under Mikhail Gorbachev still attempted to accelerate world communism and emulate the arms and military capacity of the West. But within the next four years, the Kremlin lost its empire, and its domestic and foreign policies collapsed.

Certainly there were important points in shifting the Cold War prior to 1983: the growth of the consensus in favor of increased defense spending in the late 1970s; the throttling of SALT II; the catalytic impact of Iran and Afghanistan; and the election of Ronald Reagan in 1980. The president understood the import of these factors, conveyed them to the American people, and incorporated them into his policies. While victory against the Soviets was nearer after 1983, its outline was not visible for several years. In contrast to most of the media and foreign policy experts, President Reagan knew that the triumphs of 1983 should not be translated into conciliation and compromise as the political theme of 1984.

The Beginning of the End

In sum, then, 1983 was *the* crucial year. It was the year that America conclusively demonstrated it was not in decline, as had seemed the trend at any point from 1968 on, but vigorously would defend itself and carry the fight to the Soviets. The ideological counterattack reached full voice, NATO was saved, nuclear deterrence was protected successfully from the assault of the nuclear freeze movement, the strategic defense initiative was launched, El Salvador and with it containment in Central America survived the worst that could be thrown against it, the groundwork was laid for the Reagan Doctrine, the Brezhnev Doctrine was disassembled in Grenada, and an economic expansion began that reaffirmed American prosperity for the rest of the decade. In many respects, the "Vietnam syndrome" that had prevented American vigor for a decade was dismantled, not in the Persian Gulf War of 1991, but in 1983.

These factors, including SDI, Euromissile deployment, and elements of the rhetorical counteroffensive, created what Mr. Shevardnadze later referred to as a "Gordian knot" for the Soviet leadership, which found itself at times "sinking into despair over the impasse" that ultimately would lead to a radically new policy direction. Genrikh Trofimenko, who was head of the Department for the Study of the U.S. Foreign Policy at the former Soviet Institute of the USA and Canada, similarly remarked that Mr. Reagan's strategy, and the effect it had on the Soviet regime, convinced "99 percent of all Russians that Reagan won the Cold War."

None of President Reagan's grand strategy that began to coalesce in 1983 was inevitable; in fact, every element of it was bitterly opposed and ridiculed by powerful segments of American and Western political, cultural, and intellectual opinion. And even those who believed in the policies could not know the outcome. Only the steadfast political wisdom, confidence, and determination of Ronald Reagan—and the common sense of the American citizenry—insured that America held firm. A president must join prudence and courage in the service of right principles, and he must be led by the soul of his people while being willing and able to lead their minds.

As 1980 denotes a watershed in domestic politics, 1983 is the counterpart in world politics. The year 1983—a year of extraordinary importance to the ongoing triumph of human freedom in the protracted conflict against communist totalitarianism—stands out as more than a historical marker. It is an anniversary worth noting not only for its own sake but also for the lessons it offers: history is made by human beings making choices, and in a battle for the survival of great and good principles, simply being right is not enough. Fortune favors the brave.

Reagan and Gorbachev: An Unexpected Thaw in the Cold War

John Lewis Gaddis

Reagan's initial years in office were marked by increased tensions in U.S.–Soviet relations. Reagan famously denounced the Soviet Union as an "evil empire," he supported the arms race, and his proposed Strategic Defense Initiative seemed, to the Soviets, as one more attempt to gain an edge in that contest. Thus it is a great historical irony, notes Yale historian John Lewis Gaddis in the following excerpt from his book *The United States at the End of the Cold War*, that during Reagan's second term relations between the two superpowers became warmer than they had been in over forty years.

This unexpected development, writes Gaddis, was due in no small part to the accession of the revolutionary Mikhail Gorbachev as head of the Soviet Union. But Reagan should also be given his share of the credit for these historical developments, writes Gaddis. To many people, Reagan's willingness to negotiate with the Soviets and his sincere desire to abolish nuclear weapons seemed like signs of a complete policy reversal toward the Soviets. In reality, argues Gaddis, Reagan was much less of a "hard-liner" than either his critics or his supporters thought. The president was opposed to the spread of communism but also to the proliferation of nuclear weapons; upon meeting a Soviet leader who shared many of his views, Reagan seized the opportunity to negotiate. As Gaddis explains, these negotiations culminated in the first treaty in history in which the two superpowers agreed to reduce their nuclear arsenals.

THE LAST THING ONE WOULD HAVE ANTICIPATED AT THE time Ronald Reagan took office in 1981 was that he would use his eight years in the White House to bring about the most significant improvement in Soviet-American relations since the end of World War II. I am not at all sure that President Reagan himself foresaw this result. And yet, that is precisely what happened, with—admittedly—a good deal of help from Mikhail Gorbachev. . . .

It is difficult, now, to recall how far Soviet-American relations had deteriorated at the time Ronald Reagan entered the White House. . . .

There was little visible evidence, at the time he took office, that the new president expected anything other than a renewed Cold War: indeed he went out of his way in his first White House press conference to assert that the Soviet Union had used detente as "a one-way street . . . to pursue its own aims," that those included "the promotion of world revolution and a one-world Socialist or Communist state," and that "they reserve unto themselves the right to commit any crime, to lie, to cheat, in order to attain that." . . .

Combining Militancy with Pragmatism

President Reagan in March, 1983, made his most memorable pronouncement on the Soviet Union: condemning the tendency of his critics to hold both sides responsible for the nuclear arms race, he denounced the U.S.S.R. as an "evil empire" and as "the focus of evil in the modern world." Two weeks later, the President surprised even his closest associates by calling for a long-term research and development program to create defenses against attacks by strategic missiles, with a view, ultimately, to "rendering these nuclear weapons impotent and obsolete." The Strategic Defense Initiative was the most fundamental challenge to existing orthodoxies on arms control since negotiations on that subject had begun with the Russians almost three decades earlier. Once again it called into question the President's seriousness in seeking an end to—or even a significant moderation of—the strategic arms race.

Anyone who listened to the "evil empire" speech or who considered the implications of "Star Wars" might well have concluded that Reagan saw the Soviet-American relationship as an elemental confrontation between virtue and wickedness that would allow neither negotiation nor conciliation in any form; his tone seemed more appropriate to a medieval crusade than to a revival of containment. Certainly there were those within his administration who held such views, and their influence, for a time, was considerable. But to see the President's policies solely in terms of his rhetoric, it is now clear, would have been quite wrong.

For President Reagan appears to have understood—or to have quickly learned—the dangers of basing foreign policy solely on ideology: he combined militancy with a surprising degree of operational pragmatism and a shrewd sense of timing. To the astonishment of his own hard-line supporters, what appeared to be an enthusiastic return to the Cold War in fact turned out to be a more solidly based approach to detente than anything the Nixon, Ford, or Carter administrations had been able to accomplish. . . .

The first indications that the President might be interested in something other than an indefinite arms race began to appear in the spring and summer of 1983. Widespread criticism of his "evil empire" speech apparently shook him: although his view of the Soviet system itself did not change, Reagan was careful, after that point, to use more restrained language in characterizing it. Clear evidence of the President's new moderation came with the Korean airliner incident of September, 1983. Despite his outrage, Reagan did not respond—as one might have expected him to—by reviving his "evil empire" rhetoric; instead he insisted that arms control negotiations would continue, and in a remarkably conciliatory television address early in 1984 he announced that the United States was "in its strongest position in years to establish a constructive and realistic working relationship with the Soviet Union." The President concluded this address by speculating on how a typical Soviet couple—Ivan and Anya—might find that they had much in common with a typical American couple—Jim and Sally: "They might even have decided that they were all going to get together for dinner some evening soon."...

Reagan and Gorbachev

By the end of September, 1984—and to the dismay of Democratic partisans who saw Republicans snatching the "peace" issue from them—a contrite Soviet Foreign Minister Andrei Gromyko had made the pilgrimage to Washington to re-establish contacts with the Reagan administration. Shortly after Reagan's landslide re-election over Walter Mondale in November, the United States and the Soviet Union announced that a new set of arms control negotiations would begin early the following year, linking together discussions on Strategic Arms Reductions Talks (START), Intermediate-range Nuclear Forces (INF), and weapons in space. And in December, a hitherto obscure member of the Soviet Politburo, Mikhail Gorbachev, announced while visiting Great Britain that the U.S.S.R. was prepared to seek "radical solutions" looking toward a ban on nuclear missiles altogether. Three months later, Konstantin Chernenko, the last in a series of feeble and unimaginative Soviet leaders, expired, and Gorbachev—a man who was in no way feeble and unimaginative—became the General Secretary of the Community Party of the Soviet Union. Nothing would ever be quite the same again....

Whatever the circumstances that led to it, the accession of Gorbachev reversed almost overnight the pattern of the preceding four years: after March, 1985, it was the Soviet

Union that seized the initiative in relations with the West. It did so in a way that was both reassuring and unnerving at the same time: by becoming so determinedly cooperative as to convince some supporters of containment in the United States and Western Europe—uneasy in the absence of the intransigence to which they had become accustomed—that the Russians were now seeking to defeat that strategy by depriving it, with sinister cleverness, of an object to be contained.

President Ronald Reagan and Soviet leader Mikhail Gorbachev were on friendly terms during their historic 1985 meeting in Geneva, Switzerland.

President Reagan, in contrast, welcomed the fresh breezes emanating from Moscow and moved quickly to establish a personal relationship with the new Soviet leader. Within four days of Gorbachev's taking power, the President was characterizing the Russians as "in a different frame of mind than they've been in the past. . . . [T]hey, I believe, are really going to try and, with us, negotiate a reduction in armaments." And within four months, the

White House was announcing that Reagan would meet Gorbachev at Geneva in November for the first Soviet-American summit since 1979.

The Geneva summit, like so many before it, was long on symbolism and short on substance. The two leaders appeared to get along well with one another: they behaved, as one Reagan adviser later put it, "like a couple of fellows who had run into each other at the club and discovered that they had a lot in common." The President agreed to discuss deep cuts in strategic weapons and improved verification, but he made it clear that he was not prepared to forgo development of the Strategic Defense Initiative in order to get them. His reason—which Gorbachev may not have taken seriously until this point—had to do with his determination to retain SDI as a means ultimately of rendering nuclear weapons obsolete. The President's stubbornness on this point precluded progress, at least for the moment. . . .

Working Together to Reduce the Nuclear Threat

Still, the line between rhetoric and conviction is a thin one: the first Reagan-Gorbachev summit may not only have created a personal bond between the two leaders; it may also have sharpened a vague but growing sense in the minds of both men that, despite all the difficulties in constructing an alternative, an indefinite continuation of life under nuclear threat was not a tolerable condition for either of their countries, and that their own energies might very well be directed toward overcoming that situation.

That both Reagan and Gorbachev were thinking along these lines became clear at their second meeting, the most extraordinary Soviet-American summit of the postwar era, held on very short notice at Reykjavik, Iceland, in October, 1986. . . .

A series of events set in motion by a Soviet diplomat's arrest on a New York subway platform and by the reciprocal framing of an American journalist in Moscow had wound up with the two most powerful men in the world agreeing—for the moment, and to the astonishment of their aides—on the abolition of all nuclear weapons within ten years. But the moment did not last. Gorbachev went on to insist, as a condition for nuclear abolition, upon a ban on the laboratory testing of SDI, which Reagan immediately interpreted as an effort to kill strategic defenses altogether. Because the antiballistic missile (ABM) treaty does allow for some laboratory testing, the differences between the two positions were not all that great. But in the hothouse atmosphere of this cold-climate summit no one explored such details, and the meeting broke up in disarray, acrimony, and mutual disappointment. . . .

Negotiations on arms control continued in the year that followed Reykjavik, however, with both sides edging toward the long-awaited "grand compromise" that would defer SDI in return for progress toward a START agreement. Reagan and Gorbachev did sign an intermediate-range nuclear forces treaty in Washington in December, 1987, which for the first time provided that Russians and Americans would actually dismantle and destroy—literally before each other's eyes—an entire category of nuclear missiles. There followed a triumphal Reagan visit to Moscow in May, 1988, featuring the unusual sight of a Soviet general secretary and an American president strolling amiably through Red Square, greeting tourists and bouncing babies in front of Lenin's tomb, while their respective military aides—each carrying the codes needed to launch nuclear missiles at each other's territory—stood discreetly in the background. Gorbachev made an equally triumphal visit to New York in December, 1988, to address the United Nations General Assembly: there he announced a *unilateral* Soviet cut of some 500,000 ground troops, a major step toward moving arms control into the realm of conventional forces.

When, on the same day Gorbachev spoke in New York, a disastrous earthquake killed some 25,000 Soviet Armenians, the outpouring of aid from the United States and other Western countries was unprecedented since the days of Lend Lease. One had the eerie feeling, watching anguished television reports from the rubble that had been the cities of Leninakan and Stipak—the breakdown of emergency services, the coffins stacked like logs in city parks, the mass burials—that one had glimpsed, on a small scale, something of what a nuclear war might actually be like. The images suggested just how vulnerable both super-powers remained after almost a half-century of trying to minimize vulnerabilities. They thereby reinforced what had become almost a ritual incantation pronounced by both Reagan and Gorbachev at each of their now-frequent summits: "A nuclear war cannot be won and must never be fought."

But as the Reagan administration prepared to leave office the following month, in an elegiac mood very different from the grim militancy with which it had assumed its responsibilities eight years earlier, the actual prospect of a nuclear holocaust seemed more remote than at any point since the Soviet-American nuclear rivalry had begun. Accidents, to be sure, could always happen. Irrationality, though blessedly rare since 1945, could never be ruled out. There was reason for optimism, though, in the fact that as George Bush entered the White House early in 1989, the point at issue no longer seemed to be "how to fight the Cold War" at all, but rather "is the Cold War over?"

Reagan's Role in Ending the Cold War

The record of the Reagan years suggests the need to avoid the common error of trying to predict outcomes from attributes. There is no question that the President and his advisers came into office with an ideological view of the world that appeared to allow for no compromise with the Russians; but ideology has a way of evolving to accommodate reality, especially in the hands of skillful political leadership. Indeed a good working definition 'of leadership might be just this—the ability to accommodate ideology to practical reality—and by that standard, Reagan's achievements in relations with the Soviet Union will certainly compare favorably with, and perhaps even surpass, those of Richard Nixon and Henry Kissinger.

Did President Reagan intend for things to come out this way? That question is, of course, more difficult to determine, given our lack of access to the archives. But a careful reading of the public record would, I think, show that the President was expressing hopes for an improvement in Soviet-American relations from the moment he entered the White House, and that he began shifting American policy in that direction as early as the first months of 1983, almost two years before Mikhail Gorbachev came to power. Gorbachev's extraordinary receptiveness to such initiatives—as distinct from the literally moribund responses of his predecessors—greatly accelerated the improvement in relations, but it would be a mistake to credit him solely with the responsibility for what happened: Ronald Reagan deserves a great deal of the credit as well.

Critics have raised the question, though, of whether President Reagan was responsible for, or even aware of, the direction administration policy was taking. This argument is, I think, both incorrect and unfair. Reagan's opponents have been quick enough to hold him personally responsible for the failures of his administration; they should be equally prepared to acknowledge his successes. And there are points, even with the limited sources now available, where we can see that the President himself had a decisive impact upon the course of events. They include, among others: the Strategic Defense Initiative, which may have had its problems as a missile shield but which certainly worked in unsettling the Russians; endorsement of the "zero option" in the INF talks and real reductions in

START; the rapidity with which the President entered into, and thereby legitimized, serious negotiations with Gorbachev once he came into office; and, most remarkably of all, his eagerness to contemplate alternatives to the nuclear arms race in a way no previous president had been willing to do.

Now, it may be objected that these were simple, unsophisticated, and, as people are given to saying these days, imperfectly "nuanced" ideas. I would not argue with that proposition. But it is important to remember that while complexity, sophistication, and nuance may be prerequisites for intellectual leadership, they are not necessarily so for political leadership, and can at times actually get in the way. President Reagan generally meant precisely what he said: when he came out in favor of negotiations from strength, or for strategic arms reductions as opposed to limitations, or even for making nuclear weapons ultimately irrelevant and obsolete, he did not do so in the "killer amendment" spirit favored by geopolitical sophisticates on the right; the President may have been conservative but he was never devious. The lesson here ought to be to beware of excessive convolution and subtlety in strategy, for sometimes simple-mindedness wins out, especially if it occurs in high places.

THE STRATEGIC DEFENSE INITIATIVE HELPED END THE COLD WAR

LOU CANNON

For much of the Cold War, the concept of mutually assured destruction (MAD) dominated the arms race. The basic premise was that if either the United States or the Soviets were ever to fire their nuclear missiles, the other side would still have enough time to fire theirs. Thus MAD served as a "deterrent" to nuclear war. The arms race was directly related to the concept of deterrence: Neither side wanted the other to think they could possibly win a nuclear war, so the United States and the Soviet Union each strove to maintain a nuclear arsenal that was slightly more powerful than the other's.

Not surprisingly, many people were uncomfortable with the concept of mutually assured destruction. As Lou Cannon explains in the following article, Ronald Reagan was particularly troubled by the possibility of nuclear war with the Soviets. Early in his presidency, he became fascinated with the prospect of somehow defending the United States against a nuclear attack. On March 23, 1983, in a nationally televised address, Reagan announced plans for the Strategic Defense Initiative (SDI): a space-based, computer controlled defense system that would shoot down nuclear missiles before they reached their targets. Cannon, a reporter for the *Washington Post* throughout the Reagan presidency and the author of *President Reagan: The Role of a Lifetime*, explores how the president came up with the concept of SDI. He maintains that although an actual missile defense system never materialized, the prospect of the United States

Reprinted, with permission, from Lou Cannon, "Reagan's Big Idea," *National Review*, February 22, 1999. Copyright ©1999 by National Review, Inc., www.nationalreview.com.

building such a defense helped convince the Soviets to resume arms reduction negotiations.

ON THE EVE OF RONALD REAGAN'S ELECTION AS FORTIETH president of the United States, a reporter asked him what Americans saw in him. Reagan hesitated, then replied, "Would you laugh if I told you that I think, maybe, they see themselves and that I'm one of them? I've never been able to detach myself or think that I, somehow, am apart from them."

No one laughed. Reagan was popular with the working press, and reporters found it neither immodest of him nor newsworthy that he saw himself as national Everyman. While many in the campaign press corps had from time to time been appalled by Reagan's knowledge gaps, they had also been impressed by his consistent ability to connect with the people. Reagan was then 69 years old and secure in this connection. His bond with his fellow Americans was a gift that had been nourished in Illinois and Iowa and polished in Hollywood and on the campaign trail. "Reagan's solutions to problems were always the same as the guy in the bar," said his political strategist, Stu Spencer. Walter Lippmann once wrote that the greatness of de Gaulle was not that he was in France but that France was in him. In the same sense, America was in Ronald Reagan.

Reagan's Abhorrence of Nuclear Weapons

A recognition that Reagan, while in many ways exceptional, was in truth an ordinary American helps explain his interest in the vision that became the Strategic Defense Initiative or Star Wars. (The "Star Wars" label, while intended derisively, did not harm the missile-defense cause. In the movie trilogy, as Richard Perle observed, "the good guys won.") Reagan shared not only the common sense of the "guy in the bar" but his innocence, and to some extent his ignorance of strategic issues in the nuclear age. Ordinary Americans rarely dwell on calamities too awful to contemplate such as the grim reality that the precarious peace called the Cold War was preserved by fear of mutual annihilation. After Reagan proposed SDI, polls showed that most Americans had assumed the United States possessed some defense against nuclear missiles, other than the threat of wiping out those who launched them. They were horrified, as Reagan had been, when they learned otherwise.

Running for governor of California in 1966, Reagan often said that "there are simple answers, just not easy ones." But there is no simple or single explanation for Reagan's fascination with SDI. His advocacy of missile defense was a distillation of many factors: religious beliefs that interpreted the Biblical story of Armageddon as a prophecy of nuclear war; a role in a movie as a government agent who thwarts the theft of a defensive death ray; a lifelong interest in science fiction; an enduring belief in American technological know-how; and an optimistic yearning for a benign alternative to the threat of nuclear war. It is difficult to identify the primary ingredient in this stew, but I suspect it was Reagan's revulsion at the idea of mutual assured destruction. Reagan is a moral man and MAD is immoral, however effective it was in deterring Soviet aggression in the decades after World War II. "It's like you and me sitting here in a discussion where we are each pointing a loaded gun at each other, and if you say anything wrong or I say anything wrong, we're going to pull the trigger," Reagan told me in a 1989 interview when I was working on my third book about him. "And I just thought this was ridiculous—mutual assured destruction. It really was a *mad* policy."

It is not clear when Reagan came to this view. The conventional opinion, compellingly put forth by Martin Anderson in his 1988 book, *Revolution,* is that Reagan's epiphany occurred during a July 31, 1979, visit to the headquarters of the North American Aerospace Defense Command at Cheyenne Mountain, Wyoming, when Air Force general James Hill explained that nothing could be done if the Soviets fired a missile at a U.S. city, aside from a few minutes' warning. According to Anderson, who accompanied him, Reagan was shocked. "We have spent all that money and have all that equipment and there is nothing we can do to prevent a nuclear missile from hitting us," he said on the flight back to Los Angeles.

Anderson is a reliable witness, but Reagan had also expressed concern about mutual assured destruction during his near-miss attempt to win the Republican presidential nomination in 1976. And he may have had even earlier qualms. In 1967, Gov. Reagan attended a briefing on defensive technologies at the invitation of physicist Edward Teller, who recalled in 1990 that Reagan had asked "good and fundamental questions" about nuclear policy. Reagan did not then go on record as favoring missile defense, but he was impressed by Teller, and it is quite possible that this briefing planted the seeds of an alternative doctrine to MAD.

Inspired by Movies

Garry Wills and others have suggested that the seeds of SDI were planted in Reagan's head by a 1940 film, *Murder in the Air,* the last and best of four low-budget potboilers featuring Reagan as Secret Service agent Brass Bancroft. In the movie, Bancroft thwarts a spy who is trying to steal the "inertia projector," which could shoot planes out of the sky from a distance before they could bomb the United States. As the film described it, this "new superweapon not only makes the United States invincible, but in so doing promises to become the greatest force for world peace ever discovered." Bancroft finds the stolen projector and uses it to down the plane in which the spy is trying to take the plans for the device to an unnamed enemy.

Reagan spent what he believed were the best years of his

life in Hollywood and forever after drew on his experiences in the film community for ideas and inspiration. He became an anti-Communist because of clashes with the Communists in the film industry. When he returned to Washington from Geneva in 1985 after meeting with the new Soviet leader, Gorbachev, Reagan compared arms-control negotiations with the Soviets to labor negotiations with movie producers when he was president of the Screen Actors Guild. Long after he had left Hollywood for the political stage, Reagan recalled the plots of his films, including the Bancroft series, and used them for anecdotes or analogies.

Reagan also had an avid interest in science fiction that began in the 1940s and endured throughout his presidency. The genre was preoccupied, particularly after Hiroshima, with fantastic weapons and interplanetary interventions to save the world from nuclear destruction. Reagan was a dreamer with an interest in world peace that prompted him to join the United World Federalists in 1945. He was a fan of the classic 1951 film, *The Day the Earth Stood Still,* in which an alien hero, played by Michael Rennie, comes to earth as an envoy from an advanced civilization that has curbed its warlike tendencies and uses an interplanetary police force of robots to destroy nations that resort to war. Rennie's civilization fears that earthlings will discover space travel and spread nuclear war into the galaxy. The alien's mission is to warn the nations of Earth to work together in peace or face destruction by the robotic police force—a decision left unresolved at film's end. Colin Powell believes that Reagan's proposal to share the fruits of SDI research with the Soviets derived from *The Day the Earth Stood Still.* The national-security community was aghast at the idea.

Early Resistance to Missile Defense

Missile defense was not on the nation's radar screen during the Reagan administration's early years. Reagan was out of commission for months after he was shot and nearly killed by a would-be assassin on March 30, 1981, and he focused on economic issues rather than foreign affairs when he returned to action. Until Gorbachev came along, he showed no interest in engaging any of a series of ailing Soviet leaders. But Reagan did put the United States in a position to

SDI Symbolized the Resurgence of the West

Former CIA director Robert M. Gates explains why he believes the Soviets were so upset at Reagan's plans for the Strategic Defense Initiative.

It wasn't SDI per se that frightened the Soviet leaders; after all, at best it would take many years to develop and deploy as an effective system. I think it was the *idea* of SDI and all it represented that frightened them. As they looked at the United States, they saw an America that apparently had the resources to increase defense spending dramatically and then add this program on top, and all of it while seeming hardly to break a sweat.

Meanwhile, an enfeebled Soviet leadership, presiding over a country confronting serious economic and social problems, knew they could not compete—at least not without some major changes. In my view, it was the broad resurgence of the West—symbolized by SDI— that convinced even some of the conservative members of the Soviet leadership that major internal changes were needed in the USSR. That decision, once made, set the stage for the dramatic events inside the Soviet Union over the next several years.

Robert M. Gates, *From the Shadows: The Ultimate Insider's Story of Five Presidents and How They Won the Cold War.* New York: Touchstone, 1996.

negotiate from strength by carrying out his campaign promise to increase military spending in what he said was a response to a continuing Soviet arms buildup. The U.S. increase in military spending was grist for the growing nuclear-freeze movement, which blamed Reagan for escalating U.S.-Soviet tensions. Few freeze advocates would have believed that Reagan saw the buildup as a means to the end of abolishing nuclear weapons.

The doctrine of deterrence had been in place for so long when Reagan took office that it seemed permanent. With few exceptions, the Left and Right shared the premises of deterrence, while disagreeing on the nature of the principal threat to peace. Arms-control professionals sought parity between the U.S. and Soviet nuclear arsenals but always at higher levels than before. The Soviets were then building powerful intercontinental ballistic missiles with multiple warheads at a pace that outstripped U.S. capabilities. The land-based component of the U.S. response to the buildup was the MX missile that President Carter had courageously endorsed over opposition within his own party. But Carter and defense secretary Harold Brown could not win congressional approval of an MX basing system, and Reagan and his own defense secretary, Caspar Weinberger, ran into the same problem. Renaming the MX the "Peacekeeper," as Reagan did, was no help. On December 7, 1982, the House stripped MX funds from the budget, setting in motion a chain of events that led to SDI.

In the early years of the Reagan administration, the concept of missile defense had been kept alive within the White House by an informal group of conservatives that included Anderson, Ed Meese, Richard Allen, and science advisor George Keyworth, with military advice from Karl Bendetsen and Air Force general Daniel Graham. The group was joined by William Clark after he replaced Allen as national security advisor. Congressional rejection of the MX spurred Clark's deputy and eventual successor, Robert

(Bud) McFarlane, to sound out key senators on ways of finding an acceptable basing system. The consultation led to a commission of outside experts, headed by Brent Scowcroft, which explored MX basing while McFarlane and the Joint Chiefs of Staff took a fresh look at missile defense.

"The Sting"

McFarlane, at once beleaguered and dedicated, was skeptical about the feasibility of a defensive system. But he was frustrated by the MX fiasco, believing that Reagan had raised public awareness about the proliferation of Soviet ICBMs without having anything to show for it. McFarlane reasoned that a missile-defense plan would force the Soviets to compete in multiple technologies where the United States would have the edge. This in turn might prod the Soviets into negotiations where U.S. missile defense could be bargained away for reduction in Soviet ICBMs. Because McFarlane believed the United States would be trading nothing for something, he called the idea "The Sting." McFarlane knew that Reagan did not see missile defense as a bargaining chip, but he believed the president would agree that deployment was unnecessary if the Soviets accepted massive reductions in their nuclear arsenals.

McFarlane found an ally in Admiral James Watkins, the chief of naval operations. Watkins was a nuclear engineer and a devout Catholic who had been outraged by a pastoral letter of U.S. Catholic bishops that condemned the nuclear arms race without mentioning the Soviet buildup. But as Watkins explored the issue, he began to question the morality and the wisdom of mutual assured destruction. By the time of the MX vote, he had decided that MAD was "morally distasteful" as well as "a political loser" and confided his views to McFarlane. Unknown to Watkins, Army general John Vessey, the chairman of the Joint Chiefs, had similar thoughts. When Watkins, in a partly scripted dialogue with McFarlane, advocated a new look at missile defense during Reagan's quarterly meeting with the chiefs in February 1983, he was backed by Vessey and the other chiefs. Reagan was delighted. Years later he remembered this meeting as seminal and told me that the chiefs had said the "technology of today" made possible a defensive nuclear shield. This was a stretch. The chiefs had taken note of promising defensive technologies they said ought to be explored. "We never believed in the umbrella," Watkins said in 1990. But Reagan thought that anything that could be imagined could be created. Buoyed by the meeting, he took the leap of faith into Star Wars.

On March 23, 1983, Reagan gave a nationally televised speech on "peace and national security," most of it a standard review of the Soviet military buildup and of Soviet and Cuban intelligence efforts in Central America. Near the end of the speech, he proposed the Strategic Defense Initiative—a bold pitch that had never even been discussed by the National Security Council. In a memorable passage, Reagan called on "the scientific community in our country, those who gave us nuclear weapons, to turn their great talents to the cause of mankind and world peace, to give us the means of rendering these nuclear weapons impotent and obsolete."

The Uproar over SDI

The rest, as they say, is history. Although Star Wars never went beyond a rudimentary testing stage, it changed the strategic-arms debate in ways favorable to the United States. This was not apparent in 1983 when Soviet leader Yuri Andropov was comparing Reagan to Hitler. U.S.-Soviet relations reached a low point on September 1 after a Soviet fighter shot down a Korean Air Lines jumbo jet, killing all 269 aboard, including 61 Americans.

Star Wars, meanwhile, caused consternation in Congress and the national-security community. Many congressional Democrats argued that a defensive shield was not possible while also contending that it was so destabilizing that it might prompt the Soviets to launch a first strike. These criticisms seemed contradictory on their face. Why would the Soviets be terrified by a weapon system that could not possibly work? ("Which is it, Al?" my journalist son Carl Cannon asked Al Gore, then a House member. Gore chuckled and did not answer the question.) The "wise men" of traditional deterrence scorned SDI. Writing in *Foreign Affairs* in 1984, McGeorge Bundy, George Kennan, Robert McNamara, and Gerard Smith argued that Reagan could have either new arms-control agreements or missile defense—but not both. These architects of deterrence thought Reagan unrealistic. "He was a romantic, a radical, a nuclear abolitionist," as Strobe Talbott put it. Talbott, then Washington bureau chief of *Time* and the author of influential books on arms control, led the way in drawing attention to Reagan's skimpy command of basic facts about nuclear weapons. Reagan, for instance, acknowledged that he did not understand "throw-weight" (the lifting power of a missile) and believed that cruise missiles could be used only defensively. Reagan also did not know (or had forgotten) that most Soviet missiles were land-based, which was the biggest difference between the U.S. and Soviet nuclear arsenals.

Reagan was not embarrassed by his deficiencies, and he dismissed out of hand the Soviet contention that SDI was really an offensive system in disguise. He had changed little over the years. Reagan's only conceit was his belief that he could negotiate effectively with anyone, as he demonstrated with Gorbachev at the Geneva summit in November 1985. Reagan was still enamored of science fiction. At one point, he departed from his briefing papers and told Gorbachev that the United States and the Soviet Union would cooperate if faced with an invasion from outer space. Gorbachev did not have at his fingertips the Marxist-Leninist position on collaborating with the imperialists against interplanetary invasion and made no response, confirming the president in his view that he had scored a useful point. Reagan went home happily from Geneva; later he read a 1985 novel called *Air Force One Is Haunted* in which a president aided by the friendly ghost of Franklin Roosevelt forces the Soviets to back down by deploying 390 anti-missile missiles in a system called "Umbrella."

Throughout his presidency, Reagan remained committed to SDI deployment. The 1986 Reykjavik summit (which revealed that Gorbachev, also no scientific whiz, was himself a closet nuclear abolitionist) broke up when Reagan refused to confine SDI to the laboratory. Widely seen at the time as a failure, Reykjavik was later credited as having set the stage for a subsequent treaty eliminating most intermediate-range nuclear missiles in Europe.

Star Wars Was a Success

Politically and diplomatically, Star Wars was a success. It put the nuclear-freeze movement on the defensive, brought back the Russians to strategic-arms talks they had abandoned, and may have hastened the demise of the Soviet Union. McFarlane wrote in his memoir *Special Trust* that countering SDI would have "required a substantial increase in Soviet expenditures for strategic forces at a time when the overall [Soviet] budget was stretched to the limit." He quoted Vladimir Lukhim, a former high-ranking Soviet official: "It's clear that SDI accelerated our catastrophe by at least five years." Although Reagan never agreed to trade it away, SDI became, in the words of secretary of state George Shultz, "the ultimate bargaining chip."

The idea of a scaled-down Star Wars survives. In 1999, President Clinton proposed spending $7 billion to build a "limited" missile system to protect against an accidental missile launch or attack by a rogue nation. Writing in the *Los Angeles Times* on January 11, Stansfield Turner, who was CIA director under Carter, endorsed the idea. Turner wrote that "we need to consider the costs and capabilities of defenses, not abstract arguments against them."

It is a shame that Reagan cannot know that members of the deterrence establishment who once ridiculed what they called "Star Wars" now give the proposal grudging credit. Gorbachev, at least, is not grudging. On U.S. public television last year, he said that Reagan is "really a very big person . . . a very great political leader." That was always the view of the guy in the bar.

The Strategic Defense Initiative Was a Failure

MICHAEL SCHALLER

In the following excerpt from his book *Reckoning with Reagan: America and Its Presidency in the 1980s,* University of Arizona history professor Michael Schaller takes a highly critical view of the Strategic Defense Initiative, Reagan's proposal to build a space-based weapons platform capable of shooting down incoming Soviet missiles. Although billions were spent on SDI, argues Schaller, it never really stood a chance of being built—from both a financial and technological perspective, it would have been almost impossible. Reagan got the idea for SDI from science fiction movies, claims Schaller, and was never able to grasp exactly how far-fetched the concept was. Finally, although he acknowledges that SDI alarmed the Soviets, Schaller maintains that this served to hinder arms reduction negotiations more than it helped.

R EAGAN HELD SEEMINGLY CONTRADICTORY VIEWS ABOUT nuclear war. Perhaps because of his early religious upbringing, he often referred to nuclear conflict as the manifestation of Armageddon, a biblical prophesy of the destruction of the world. Since he maintained that the Bible foretold all events, this presumably meant he expected an unavoidable war. Still, the prospect of such a holocaust horrified him.

During a tour in 1979 of the Strategic Air Command

Excerpted from *Reckoning with Reagan: America and Its Presidency in the 1980s,* by Michael Schaller. Copyright ©1992 by Oxford University Press, Inc. Used by permission of Oxford University Press, Inc.

center at Cheyenne Mountain in Colorado, he was shocked when told that if the Soviets fired even one missile, the United States could do nothing but track it and fire back. His friend Martin Anderson quoted Reagan as saying "we have spent all that money and have all that equipment, and there is nothing we can do to prevent a nuclear missile from hitting us." Reagan especially disliked the chilling acronym—MAD, or Mutual Assured Destruction—that described American strategy.

A Far-Fetched Solution

The president's idea of a solution to the nuclear threat stemmed partly, like many of his notions, from the movies. In the otherwise forgettable 1940 adventure film *Murder in the Air*, secret agent Brass Bancroft (Ronald Reagan) foiled the effort of foreign agents to steal a secret "inertia projector," a device that could stop enemy aircraft from flying. As one of the characters remarks, it would "make America invincible in war and therefore the greatest force for peace ever invented." Reagan often recalled the early 1950s film *The Day the Earth Stood Still* in which an alien from another planet stops all machines on Earth as a warning to mankind to seek peace.

During the late-1970s physicist Dr. Edward Teller and retired Air Force Lt. General Daniel Graham, who headed a group called High Frontier, impressed Reagan with talk of an anti-missile shield. During a 1983 meeting in the Oval Office, Teller told Reagan about progress in building an X-ray laser powered by a nuclear bomb. In theory, the device could produce energy beams capable of shooting down Soviet missiles after their launch and before they deployed their multiple warheads. Mounted on orbiting platforms, they could provide a space shield, or "astrodome," over America. As Teller expected, the president liked the idea of a high technology "fix" and neglected to probe for details.

In March 1983, when Reagan unveiled his updated secret weapon, his words paraphrased those spoken in his 1940 film. The president revealed a startling vision of a peaceful future in which a "Strategic Defense Initiative" (SDI) would render nuclear weapons "impotent and obsolete." Reagan proposed a vast research and development program to develop an anti-missile system. Most critics, and many supporters, dubbed the concept "Star Wars."

Criticisms and Doubts

Only a handful of White House insiders knew in advance of Reagan's initiative. The Joint Chiefs of Staff and the secretaries of state and defense were skeptics, while National Security Adviser Robert McFarlane favored SDI as a bargaining chip with the Soviets rather than as an actual system. However, the White House public relations staff had been consulted more closely. Michael Deaver arranged for testing the idea on focus groups and found solid support for a "space shield." Deaver admitted he and those queried had no idea how such a shield would work but that they liked "the concept."

Many people inside and outside the administration worried that SDI violated the [anti-ballistic missile] (ABM) treaty, which barred the United States and Soviet Union from testing or deploying any new anti-missile systems. A majority of scientists doubted that Star Wars, which depended on many types of untested technology, would ever work. Even a shield 90% effective would allow through enough enemy warheads to obliterate this country. Some critics judged SDI little more than a fig leaf to mask substantial assistance for American companies engaged in high technology competition against Japan. For example, the Rockwell Corporation issued a promotional brochure for investors describing SDI as a vast new "Frontier for Growth, Leadership and Freedom." Other critics of the program speculated that SDI proponents did not really expect to shoot down missiles, but wanted to provoke Moscow into a bankrupting high technology contest.

The space shield described by the president and advertised on television by groups such as High Frontier never stood a chance of being built. The huge costs and daunting technical problems compelled weapons researchers to concentrate on developing systems to protect American *nuclear missile silos*, not cities or civilians, against a Soviet nuclear strike. They reasoned that SDI might knock out enough incoming warheads to permit sufficient American missiles to survive and launch a punishing retaliatory blow. This likelihood, presumably, would deter the Soviets from attacking. In effect, SDI would do little more than enhance, at great cost, the MAD strategy.

From Moscow's perspective, SDI appeared as one more threat. For example, the United States might launch a nuclear first strike that would destroy most Soviet missiles in their silos. An SDI anti-missile system might be good enough to shoot down a small Soviet retaliatory barrage. American leaders, confident of escaping destruction, might be tempted to initiate nuclear war under these conditions.

An Expensive Failure

Between 1983 and 1989, the United States spent almost $17 billion on SDI research, but achieved few results. The much-touted X-ray laser failed to work and the estimated cost of even a limited space shield literally skyrocketed. The disappointing record of the space shuttle left the United States with little ability to even carry components of SDI into space. A decade after the president unveiled the scheme, it remained a distant prospect.

The Reagan Military Buildup Prolonged the Cold War

Raymond L. Garthoff

Many conservative commentators have been quick to argue that Ronald Reagan "won" the Cold War. According to this view, the Soviet economy was too poor to win an extended arms race with the United States; with this in mind, the Reagan administration supported a military buildup and increased its efforts to fight Communist expansion in Third World countries. The Soviet Union, unable to match this increased show of U.S. force, eventually agreed to arms reductions in 1987, and in 1989, to release its hold on the nations of Eastern Europe.

In the following article, Raymond L. Garthoff, a former ambassador to Bulgaria and a senior fellow at the Brookings Institute, rejects this thesis. He maintains that Mikhail Gorbachev, not Ronald Reagan, was primarily responsible for ending the Cold War. Immediately after Gorbachev came to power, he sought to reform a corrupt Soviet system, institute liberal reforms in Eastern Europe, and improve relations with the West. These efforts, writes Garthoff, were hindered rather than helped by the military posturing of the Reagan administration, because they made it harder for Gorbachev to convince his government to trust the United States. Garthoff concludes that Reagan helped to end the Cold War—rather than prolong it—only in the final years of his presidency, when he began to trust Gorbachev and work to help him achieve his goals.

Reprinted with permission from *Insight* from Raymond L. Garthoff, "Did the Reagan Doctrine Cause the Fall of the Soviet Union? No: Give Credit to Mikhail Gorbachev's Decisive Steps to End the Cold War," *Insight*, January 26, 1998. Copyright 1998 News World Communications, Inc. All rights reserved.

D ID THE REAGAN ADMINISTRATION'S CONFRONTATIONAL posture and its attendant military buildup force Soviet leaders into an intensified arms race they could not keep up with, eventually bringing the Soviet Union into economic crisis? Did it compel Soviet global retreat and retraction of its military and political power from Europe? Was a vigorous push beyond containment the secret to bringing the Cold War to an end? No, not to the extent frequently argued.

Despite the Jimmy Carter–Ronald Reagan military buildup from 1980–85, continuing thereafter at a high but no longer increasing level, according to Central Intelligence Agency–Defense Intelligence Agency figures Soviet military expenditures continued until about 1985 at a reduced level of growth set in the mid-1970s. There then was some increase in 1985–88, partly catch-up, partly to maintain a level of military expenditures offsetting incipient general economic decline.

The Reagan Military Buildup Fueled Soviet Suspicions

In general, it appears that the Soviets reacted to the U.S. buildup by delaying their reductions in military expenditures. As soon as internal political maneuver allowed, Mikhail Gorbachev began radical cuts in the Soviet military establishment and a major reduction in military spending in 1989–91, notwithstanding continuing high U.S. military outlays.

As for Reagan's Strategic Defense Initiative, also known as SDI or Star Wars, its main impact was to persuade Yuri Andropov and many in the Soviet political and military leadership that the United States would seek to press its growing military advantage politically, to undercut Soviet deterrence and possibly even to threaten military attack. Star Wars certainly helped to hold back any Soviet reduction in military spending in the mid-1980s.

Contrary to a widely held impression, however, Star Wars did not force the Soviet Union into major new expenditures. The decision was made in Moscow to meet any SDI programs if and as a concrete military threat became real, and then through appropriate, less costly, offsetting asymmetric countermeasures. Studies were undertaken, but not new military programs. As a concrete military-technological challenge, SDI never was sufficiently defined to permit creating and procuring countermeasures.

SDI did not help the cause of arms control. It made it harder for Gorbachev to persuade the Soviet military leaders to make deep reductions in strategic arms, inasmuch as some countermeasures might depend upon strategic missiles. Nonetheless, he persisted. As soon as his internal political position permitted, Gorbachev went ahead with substantial reductions in military spending despite a continuing, if attenuated, U.S. Star Wars program.

There was a broader negative aspect to the impact of the Reagan military buildup and confrontational line in 1981–83. The open enmity of Reagan and his first-term administration reinforced the Marxist-Leninist stereotype of hostile imperialist designs, making it more difficult for Soviet leaders to see the falsity of their ideological conceptions of the world.

Moreover, the Reagan administration also secretly engaged in acts of military intimidation. Only recently has it begun to become known that in addition to aggressive, stepped-up naval and air reconnaissance along Soviet borders, naval exercises included secret approaches to Soviet waters and flights of bombers toward Soviet territory, turning away only at the last moment. These provocative actions were most intensive in 1981–83 but continued in some respects at least into 1986. The most dangerous moment occurred in November 1983, when Andropov and his intelligence chiefs even believed the United States might start a nuclear war, incredible as that seems.

One unexpected consequence of the Reagan military buildup was, paradoxically, to persuade some Soviet leaders that no country, not even the wealthy United States, could afford to spend endlessly on a military buildup that did not really yield any military or political dividends or options. Perhaps the Soviet Union could not match the U.S. military and military-technological buildup, but the most important thing they learned was that it didn't need to.

Gorbachev the Reformer

Gorbachev set out in 1985–86 to end the arms race and the Cold War. His aims, and even the path to achieve them, although daunting, were clearer to him than the way to realize his aims in internal *perestroika*. He could not, of course, do everything that he wanted to at once, but he set out to do it. His opening salvo was the proposal in January 1986 to eliminate nuclear weapons in a decade. After the summits at Geneva, Switzerland, in 1985 and Reykjavik, Iceland, in 1986, Gorbachev believed there was a real possibility to work with Reagan, but he also saw that the Soviet Union would have to assume the main burden of turning down the arms race. Equal security and equal reductions would have to give way to more Soviet initiative and to greater Soviet concessions, not concessions compelled by Western political pressure or the economic pressure of the arms race, but concessions to reality. The Intermediate-range Nuclear Forces Treaty was concluded in 1987, and both a first Strategic Arms Reduction Treaty and a Treaty on Conventional Forces in Europe were signed by 1990 after major Soviet concessions.

But along the way there also had to be unilateral reductions and a unilateral start of withdrawal of Soviet forces from Eastern Europe, both announced in December 1988.

Gorbachev's actions were not responsive to the Reagan push and arms buildup or caused by it; they came despite it, to serve the more important objective of ending the arms race, the military confrontation and the Cold War. Gorbachev didn't lose the arms race; he just opted out.

Gorbachev's internal liberalization, his *glasnost* and *demokratizatsiya,* also was not responsive to the Carter-Reagan push on democratization and human rights, but despite it. His liberalization of relations with Eastern Europe, begun in 1985–86, also was pursued despite U.S. propaganda and, in some cases, especially in Poland, covert operations. Gorbachev's initiative in revoking the Brezhnev Doctrine not only was not the product of Western pressure, it was long the object of Western suspicion and disbelief. While the West still was juggling asymmetrical mutual and balanced force-reduction proposals for conventional arms reductions, Gorbachev preempted with even larger unilateral cuts.

Gorbachev's drawdown of support for Third World clients also advanced despite the push of the Reagan Doctrine, not because of it, although U.S. aid to insurgencies did increase the cost burden. The decision to pull out of Afghanistan, for example, was made in late 1985, a year before the first U.S. stinger missiles arrived. Moreover, it proceeded despite Reagan's repudiation of an earlier U.S. commitment to cease supplying the mujahideen rebels after the Soviet withdrawal.

Some of Gorbachev's actions could be explained as retrenchments from overextended positions, if not in response to U.S. pressures, in particular the decision to withdraw from Afghanistan. But Gorbachev was under no pressure at all to undertake unilateral cuts in conventional forces or to take the initiative in giving up all Warsaw Pact numerical superiorities in forces, tanks, artillery and aircraft, and later to accede readily to Czechoslovakian and Hungarian requests to withdraw all Soviet forces in short order. Some of these actions cost the Soviet Union heavily in economic dislocation with rapid redeployment and downsizing.

Reagan's Courageous Decision to Accept Gorbachev

Reagan and U.S. policy, to be sure, played a role in the process of winding down the Cold War, an important role; in fact, two roles. First was the pressure and push of 1981–83 (and continuing thereafter in the Third World), for better or worse (and I believe that has to be a net judgment, because it included both positive and negative impacts). Reagan's second, and I believe more important, role was

The Cold War Ended *Despite* the Reagan Military Buildup

Gorbachev's withdrawal of Soviet forces from Afghanistan, proposals for arms control, and domestic reforms took place *despite* the Reagan buildup. Mikhail Sergeyevich Gorbachev came to power in March 1985 committed to liberalizing the domestic political process at home and improving relations with the West so that the Soviet Union could modernize its rigid economy. Within a month of assuming office, he announced his first unilateral initiative—a temporary freeze on the deployment of Soviet intermediate-range missiles in Europe—and in a series of subsequent proposals tried to signal his interest in arms control. President Reagan continued to speak of the Soviet Union as an "evil empire" and remained committed to his quest for a near-perfect ballistic-missile defense.

Gorbachev came to office imbued with a sense of urgency of domestic reform and with a fundamentally different attitude toward the West. He was confident that the United States would not deliberately attack the Soviet Union and that the serious risk was an acciden-

his later courageous readiness to accept Gorbachev's moves. It was, above all, the Reagan of 1986–88 that helped to end the Cold War. It was Reagan's easing off of the arms buildup, military intimidation and hostile rhetorical policy of confrontation that facilitated Gorbachev's sharp cut in military spending after 1988, not the earlier Reagan military buildup when Leonid Brezhnev, Yuri Andropov and Konstantin Chernenko were in power. President Bush then helped Gorbachev to cushion the impact of Soviet with-

tal or miscalculated exchange. In conversations with his military advisors, he rejected any plans that were premised on a war with the United States. . . . Since he saw no threat of attack from the United States, Gorbachev was not "afraid" of any military programs put forward by the Reagan administration and did not feel forced to match them. Rather, he saw arms spending as an unnecessary and wasteful expenditure of scarce resources. Deep arms reductions were not only important to the reform and development of the Soviet economy, but also an imperative of the nuclear age.

Rather than facilitating a change in Soviet foreign policy, Reagan's commitment to the Strategic Defense Initiative (SDI) complicated Gorbachev's task of persuading his own officials that arms control was in the Soviet interest. Conservatives, much of the military leadership, and captains of defense-related industries took SDI as further evidence of the hostile intentions of the United States and insisted on increasing spending on offensive countermeasures.

Richard Ned Lebow and Janice Gross Stein, "The Myth of Deterrence and the End of the Cold War," in *Myth America, Volume II*, Patrick Gertser and Nicholas Cords, eds. St. James, NY: Brandywine Press, 1997.

drawal from Eastern and Central Europe in 1989–90. The Cold War came to an end during the year from the opening of the Berlin Wall to the celebration in the November 1990 Paris Charter of the reunification of Germany, of Europe and, in a sense, of the world.

Claims that Reagan and his hard-line confrontational stance of the early 1980s brought the Soviet Union to its knees a few years later give him too much, and too little, credit: too much for any positive effect of that image, but too little for the Reagan who, in 1988 in Moscow, declared that he no longer believed the Soviet Union was an evil empire and acknowledged that his remarks to that effect a few years earlier had concerned another time, another era. As, indeed, they had.

The main factor is that Gorbachev came to power and acted to bring the Cold War to an end. If he had not, the history of the 1980s and the 1990s would have been different. At the same time, paradoxically, although Gorbachev succeeded in bringing down traditional communist rule, he failed in his efforts to restructure a more humanistic socialism and voluntary renewed union; if he had not come to power the Soviet Union probably still would be with us today.

The Cold War rested squarely on the belief on both sides that two ideological and geopolitical systems were locked in an inescapable struggle to the finish. And that belief, in turn, rested on the Marxist-Leninist worldview positing an inevitable struggle for world hegemony between two irreconcilable contending socioeconomic (class), political, geopolitical and military systems.

Only when a Soviet leadership was able to recognize that such a worldview was false and to act on the basis of rejection of that worldview could leaders of the United States and the West accept (at first cautiously) the possibility of moving, in Bush's words, beyond containment. The guiding U.S. Cold War conception of containment of the Soviet and world communist threat was derivative of and dependent on the Soviet belief in inescapable conflict between two systems. Only when a Soviet leader saw and repudiated the fallacious foundation for the Cold War could Western leaders see that containment of a no longer extant communist threat to the free world no longer was necessary. Gorbachev, aided by Reagan and Bush, brought the Cold War to an end.

PRESIDENTS *and their* DECISIONS

CHAPTER

3

The Iran-Contra Affair

THE REAGAN ADMINISTRATION'S INVOLVEMENT IN CENTRAL AMERICA

HAYNES JOHNSON

The Iran-contra affair consisted of two different operations. The first was the Reagan administration's sale of arms to Iran, part of an attempt to gain the release of hostages being held by terrorist groups in that country. As the name suggests, the second part of the Iran-contra affair involved America's support for the contradistas, or contras, a group of Nicaraguan "freedom fighters" who opposed the Sandinistas, the Marxist government that had come to power in that country.

President Reagan and his staff were very concerned about the possibility of Nicaragua becoming a base for communist expansion in Central America. They feared that if communism were to spread from Nicaragua to El Salvador, it would eventually spread north to Mexico, and the Soviet Union would have allies that shared a border with the United States. To prevent this, the Reagan administration sought to provide military aid to the government of El Salvador, and later to the Nicaraguan rebel group, the contradistas. However, because the government of El Salvador at the time was a dictatorship, and because many Americans dreaded the prospect of "another Vietnam" in Central America, in 1982 and 1984 Congress passed the Boland amendments, which prohibited any further aid to the Nicaraguan rebels. The Reagan administration's illegal attempt to circumvent these congressional orders was a key part of the Iran-contra scandal.

Excerpted from *Sleepwalking Through History: America in the Reagan Years*, by Haynes Johnson. Copyright ©1991 by Haynes Johnson. Used by permission of W.W. Norton & Company, Inc.

In the following excerpt from his book *Sleepwalking Through History: America in the Reagan Years*, Haynes Johnson, a Pulitzer Prize–winning reporter for the *Washington Post*, explains why the Reagan administration was so adamant in its desire to aid El Salvador and the contras.

I N HIS LAST DAYS IN OFFICE CARTER CANCELED AID TO Nicaragua. The military offensive in El Salvador, coming on the eve of a shift in power in Washington, triggered a new version of the old domino theory debate in the United States: One by one the Central American states would fall until the entire area was under the control of Marxist-Leninist regimes backed by the Soviet Union and its Caribbean proxy, Cuba.

This was the situation that greeted a new president who had promised to stop communism, to restore U.S. military might and prestige, and who had run on a Republican platform that singled out as a special danger to U.S. interests "the Marxist Sandinista takeover of Nicaragua and the Marxist attempts to destabilize El Salvador, Guatemala, and Honduras." The Republican platform plank had condemned Jimmy Carter's offer of aid to the Sandinistas. It had also pledged to "support the efforts of the Nicaraguan people to establish a free and independent government." These were more than presidential campaign rhetorical pledges. Ronald Reagan believed them. He intended to act.

Reagan's Anticommunism

Fear that Central America could become another Vietnam and a more menacing base to spread Marxism throughout the hemisphere coincided with the ideological imperatives of the Reagan administration. However else Reagan would ultimately be judged for the wisdom of his presidential decisions, there was no doubt that he came to office holding sincere and strong convictions about the dangers of communism—and of the use of force to combat it.

For Reagan, anticommunism was an article of faith. His was the most ideologically motivated American presidency of the twentieth century, and he and his key aides were determined to act in what they believed to be in the nation's best interests. The circumstances of his election and the mood of the country strengthened their resolve. Undeniably, the long hostage ordeal and cumulative public sense of American weakness gave those in the Reagan group a stronger hand to play. They had every reason to conclude that Americans wanted to recapture a feeling of national strength and success and wanted them to act forcefully when challenged. It was by no means clear, though, that Americans of the post-Vietnam period wanted them to employ U.S. combat arms to overthrow or contain Communist regimes. In fact, public opinion survey evidence suggested the opposite: that Americans did not favor new military adventures that could entrap the nation in another Vietnam.

Intellectually Reagan's views on combating communism and terrorism *were* fundamentally different from those of Carter and numerous foreign policy experts who had served a number of presidents of both parties since World War II. The Reagan world view was expressed by Jeane Kirkpatrick, whom he appointed U.S. ambassador to the United Nations. She was a political science professor and former liberal Democratic supporter of her fellow Minnesotan Hubert Humphrey. Like Reagan and many others, Kirkpatrick had turned ideological conservative— or neoconservative—by the eighties. In a celebrated essay that had attracted Reagan's personal attention and praise the year before the election, she drew distinctions between the rulers of "authoritarian" and "totalitarian" governments. Good ones (authoritarians)—Nicaragua's Somoza, the shah of Iran—preserved "traditional" societies and encouraged capitalism and the profit motive. Bad ones (totalitarians)—Hitler, Stalin—ruled by iron force and controlled every aspect of a nation's political, social, military, and economic life. Such thinking became central in the policy-making rationale of the new administration.

It was against this backdrop that Reagan and his poli-

The Constitution Limits the President's Ability to Dictate Foreign Policy

Many of Reagan's supporters felt that the Boland amendments, which specifically made it illegal for the U.S. government to provide military aid to the contras, were an unconstitutional limit on presidential authority. In the following excerpt, Martin Anderson, who served as an adviser in the Reagan administration, rebuts this argument.

The Constitution is particularly instructive in the area of foreign policy. Written in the summer of 1787, the writers could scarcely have imagined the world of nuclear superpowers and terrorist states that we live with today. Yet they are very clear on the prerogatives and powers of Congress in relationship to the chief executive, the president. When the founding fathers wrote the Constitution they had a healthy and wise distrust of *any* chief executive.

By the words of the Constitution, Congress, not the president, was given the power to:

• Regulate commerce with foreign nations.

• Define and punish piracies and felonies committed on the high seas, and offences against the law of nations.

• Declare war and make rules concerning captures on land and water.

• Raise and support armies.

cy advisers began grappling with the immediate problem they faced in Central America, specifically in El Salvador. They were determined both to set a strong new example of U.S. willingness to meet force with force and not to permit a failure in their first foreign policy challenge. . . .

Within weeks of taking office, Reagan increased aid to El Salvador fivefold. He immediately approved twenty mil-

- Provide and maintain a navy.
- Make rules for the government and regulation of the land and naval forces.
- Provide for calling forth the militia.
- Ratify all foreign treaties.
- Veto ambassadors to foreign countries.
- Appropriate money from the treasury.

They didn't leave the president out of it all together. The Constitution names him the commander-in-chief of the army and the navy, and gives him the "power, by and with the advice and consent of the Senate, to make treaties," provided two-thirds of the senators present concur. He also gets to nominate, "and by and with the advice and consent of the Senate," to appoint ambassadors to foreign countries.

And that's it. . . .

The president is preeminent in the field of foreign policy when it comes to talking. He speaks for the United States. But when it comes to fighting, Congress takes over. The enormous military power of the United States—the power of billions of dollars and sophisticated, powerful weapons and millions of combat-ready troops—has never been entrusted to the whims of any president, no matter how beloved or trusted.

Martin Anderson, *Revolution: The Reagan Legacy.* Stanford, CA: Hoover Institution Press, 1990.

lion dollars for shipment of arms and equipment there, sent additional U.S. military advisers to train Salvadoran forces fighting the rebels, arranged for additional millions in loan guarantees, and requested another twenty-five million dollars for more arms purchases.

Fifteen hundred Salvadoran soldiers were brought to the United States for special training in American military bases. The flow of arms, equipment, and economic aid increased monthly. By the end of 1982 the United States had sent more aid to El Salvador than to any other Latin American nation in that period of Reagan's presidency. While the focus was on El Salvador, the Reagan administration continued to condemn the Sandinistas and apply increasing public pressure on them. Days after the inauguration the United States publicly demanded that Nicaragua stop helping "their revolutionary brothers" in El Salvador and step away from their growing ties with Havana and Moscow. Economic screws were tightened. Fifteen million dollars in U.S. economic aid to Managua was halted. Millions of dollars of wheat shipments bound for Nicaragua were stopped. Breadlines sprang up throughout the country. Within months all U.S. aid to Nicaragua had stopped.

By then, in a major shift of U.S. foreign policy objectives in the post World War II era, the Reagan administration had elevated Central America into the nation's preeminent national security concern. Just two months after the inauguration Jeane Kirkpatrick, in a speech before the Conservative Political Action Conference, explained why Central America and the Caribbean had become "the most important place in the world for us." Echoing concerns expressed by [Secretary of State Alexander M.] Haig, she warned that failure to stop the spread of communism there would affect America's ability to play "a major role in the politics and security of countries in remote places and even Western Europe." The very security of the United States, she maintained, depended upon "not having to devote the lion's share of our attention and our resources to the defense of ourselves in our own hemisphere."

Here was a new and more threatening version of the domino theory come home to imperil the nation through America's backyard. And now the threat was occurring on Ronald Reagan's presidential watch.

An Insider's Perspective on the Iranian Initiative

Edwin Meese III

Edwin Meese III first served as a presidential adviser within the Reagan administration, and later as attorney general. When the Iran-contra affair first surfaced in November 1986, Reagan appointed Meese to quickly investigate the affair and brief him on what had occurred. Meese later described his experiences in the White House in his book *With Reagan: The Inside Story*.

In the following excerpt from that book, Meese argues that the Iran part of the Iran-contra affair was not illegal. The president never sought to trade arms for hostages, argues Meese, but was instead trying to develop better relations with some of the more U.S.-friendly elements in Iran. Moreover, he believes that outside observers are too quick to assume that all aspects of the Iran-contra affair involved illegal operations. In fact, he argues, the Iranian initiative was not illegal. Instead, Reagan and his staff were careful to follow the letter of the law in every step of the way.

W AS THE PRESIDENT SIMPLY PAYING RANSOM TO HOSTAGE-takers? Few notions about the complex events of the Iran-Contra dispute have been more frequently repeated, yet few are more obviously refuted by the evidence.

Throughout the Iran initiative, both in 1985 when it was being handled by the Israelis and in 1986 when the United States handled it directly, the President stressed that we were dealing, not with the Hizballah extremists who had seized the hostages, but with third parties who had influence on them. He repeated this statement, over and over, but his opponents chose just as doggedly to ignore it.

In this respect . . . the example of the Beirut airport crisis of June 1985 is instructive. In that episode, the United States dealt with the governments of Syria and Iran to obtain the release of hostages held by extremist groups on whom these countries had some sort of influence. Those efforts ultimately proved successful—the hostages were released, the governments of Syria and Iran were thanked, and no one accused the President of dealing directly with the hostage-takers.

The President's experience in that episode clearly shaped his response to the negotiations of 1985 and 1986. In these later cases, the contacts of the United States were not with the people who took the hostages, but with people who presumably had some leverage over them—that is, the exact same configuration as at the Beirut airport. . . .

Seeking an Opening to Iran

President Reagan contended that we were trying to get an opening to "moderate" or anti-Khomeini forces in Iran rather than trafficking with hard-line terrorists and extremists. This explanation, too, has been dismissed as a subterfuge on the grounds that "all the moderates in Iran are dead." Again, the evidence strongly supports the President's view.

The idea of seeking an opening to Iran—of trying to identify and deal with moderate elements there—predated the events that brought the hostage issue to the forefront. This theme emerged time and again in early statements from the NSC [National Security Council] and CIA and were prominent in administration thinking throughout the Iranian initiative. And the President himself consistently stressed that he sought an opening to moderate elements in Tehran.

Reflecting on the August 1985 decision to approve the Israeli TOW shipments, for instance, the President wrote: "The transaction was to be solely between Israel and the Iranian moderates and would not involve our country, although we would have to waive for Israel our policy prohibiting any transfer of American-made weapons to Iran."

Reagan's Intentions Were Honorable

Many of Reagan's supporters have argued that, whatever the legality of the Iran-contra operations, throughout the affair Reagan did what he thought was right. Former secretary of state George P. Shultz echoes this view:

Iran-contra, of course, got a huge amount of attention—I think overattention. It wasn't like Watergate; Watergate had a rancid element. The things people did—even the things Casey and company did—they did for what they thought were the best interests of the United States. They were trying to fight the Communists in Central America, and they went about it in the wrong way, in a way that was not in accord with our Constitution, so it was wrong.

And Reagan's motives were, in a sense, good motives. He was worried about those Americans and wanted to get them back. The method was not a good method, but the intentions were honorable.

Quoted in Peter Hannaford, ed., *Recollections of Reagan: A Portrait of Ronald Reagan.* New York: William Morrow, 1997.

Bud McFarlane's recollection of this decision tells the same story. "The President's points," he testified, "were foremostly that he could imagine that these people in Iran were legitimate in their interest of changing Iranian policy, and were against terrorism, that to provide them with arms would not be at variance with his policy, since he wasn't providing arms to Khomeini, but to people opposed to Khomeini's policy.". . .

How realistic were such efforts? Despite frequent statements that the President was deluding himself about the existence of dissident elements in Iran, plentiful data suggest he was correct. Iran under the ayatollah was not a monolithic place, with everyone marching in lockstep to a common policy, but a cockpit of warring factions. There were a number of competing groups, with different political views and conflicting attitudes about the long-term relationship with America. . . .

The existence of these factions, the competition among them, and the shifting alliances that resulted made it difficult for us to know with whom we were dealing, whether they were reliable, and whether they could deliver what they promised. The difficulty was compounded by our lack of intelligence from Iran, a weakness that had blindsided us to the uprising against the shah and made us dependent on the advice of such middlemen as Manucher Ghorbanifar, whose contacts inside Iran were recommended by the Israelis.

Complexities notwithstanding, these different elements did exist, and some of them wanted a better relationship with America. It was therefore hardly outrageous to seek out some kind of opening to them, however difficult the problems of intelligence. . . .

The Iranian Initiative Was Legal

But, whatever its merits as policy, was such an initiative legal? By far the most serious accusation against the President was that his attempted dealings with Iran, the arms sales in particular, were unlawful. Such a charge is far more serious, of course, than a simple policy disagreement. Yet it has been lightly bandied about in our political debates, with precious little to back it up.

The notion that there was something illegal about the

initiative stems largely from two factors: (1) It was a covert activity. This meant it was never debated fully or clearly explained to Congress or the American public and gave rise to suspicions that there was something disreputable about it. Such accusations were frequently made in the aftermath of the November 1986 disclosures. One of my chief regrets was that, in its defensive reaction, the administration never made the legal and policy basis for the initiative clear; (2) The initiative was linked, via Ollie North, to the diversion of funds to the Nicaraguan resistance. (Views differ about whether the diversion itself involved criminal liability; and to date, no one has been convicted of such an offense.) . . .

In point of fact, the conduct of the White House in carrying out the Iran initiative was legal at every step along the way. To understand this, it is necessary to consider the laws applicable to the situation, something the critics of the administration seldom bother to do. These topics were carefully discussed in the Oval Office on January 7, 1986, and at subsequent meetings, and subjected to considerable research by CIA counsel Stanley Sporkin and myself. In addition, prior research on these matters had been conducted by Davis Robinson, legal counsel to the State Department, and by my predecessor at Justice, William French Smith.

Two kinds of statutes were relevant to the situation: those pertaining to the transfer of arms by the United States and countries who were recipients of U.S. weapons, and those pertaining to covert activities by the CIA. In the first instance, the Arms Export Control Act (AECA) required that any direct or indirect transfer of U.S. arms (as, for instance, by Israel), amounting to $14 million or more in terms of acquisition costs, required submission of an unclassified notice to Congress before the shipment could go forward.

An alternative route to arms transfers lay in the so-called Economy Act, which allowed the CIA to obtain weapons at cost from the Defense Department for subsequent resale in pursuit of covert activities. This triggered the requirements of the 1974 Hughes-Ryan Amendment to the National Security Act, which says that before the CIA engages in such activity the President must find it in the national interest and report the finding "in timely fashion" to the relevant committees of Congress.

In our discussions of the 1986 Iran initiative, we concluded that the Economy Act was the way to go, because it did not involve the advance, unclassified notification that would have jeopardized the security of the operation. . . .

Under the AECA, U.S. approval was required for Israeli shipments of U.S.-origin equipment to Iran. As determined by all investigations of this topic, such approval was given orally by President Reagan (as will be discussed more fully in a moment), which satisfied this requirement of the law. As for notification, neither shipment amounted to a value of $14 million in terms of acquisition costs and therefore was not covered by the statute. . . .

The Hughes-Ryan Amendment says that CIA funds may not be expended on covert operations, as opposed to intelligence activities per se, "unless and until the President finds that each such operation is important to the national security of the United States." The involvement of the CIA in this activity included no operational role and the expenditure of no intelligence funds. Against that backdrop, it is questionable whether the help provided by the CIA rose to the level that would require a presidential finding. . . .

Notifying Congress

Still another legal question that has been raised concerns the failure to provide notification of this finding to Congress. To understand the issue of disclosure, it is important to note the environment in which these activities were occurring, and the constitutional-legal obligations of the President in dealing with that environment. It is no exaggeration to say that during this period a veritable Niagara of "leaks" threatened our intelligence activities, particularly those pertaining to terrorism in the Middle East and our attempts to cope with it. . . .

Obviously, leaks had become a way of life in Washington and the probability that anything provided to Congress would *not* wind up on the front page of the *Washington Post* was remote. For those who say, "too bad, the President has to provide the notification anyway," the short answer is "no, he does not." The President takes a solemn oath to protect and defend the United States and is not required, either constitutionally or legally, to countenance the hemorrhaging of national security secrets.

Such considerations, as it happens, are recognized even in the disclosure provision of Hughes-Ryan, which says that notification must occur "to the extent consistent with due regard for the protection from unauthorized disclosure of classified information and information relating to intelligence sources and methods.". . .

The disclosure requirement under Hughes-Ryan . . . explicitly envisioned the possibility of notification *after the fact*. It states that the President shall inform the intelligence committees "in timely fashion" concerning covert activities "for which prior notice was not given." This language obviously contemplates the need for secrecy before or during the course of such activity with *ex post facto* notification to Congress, while leaving the question of timeliness open to construction. . . .

A Policy Error, Not a Crime

In retrospect, I believe that when it became apparent that the Iranian initiative was not succeeding, it should have been dropped and Congress should have been notified of what had happened. I therefore do not defend the protracted failure to disclose—but it was a policy error, not a crime. And it is worth recalling that when much the same thing happened under Jimmy Carter, the public reaction was very different. As the minority report of the Iran-Contra committees observes:

"According to Admiral Stansfield Turner, who was Director of Central Intelligence at the time, there were three occasions, all involving Iran, in which the Carter administration withheld notification [from Congress] for about three months until six Americans could be smuggled out of the Canadian embassy in Tehran. . . . Notification was also withheld for about six months in two other Iranian operations during the hostage crisis. Said Turner: 'I would have found it very difficult to look . . . a person in the eye and tell him or her that I was going to discuss this life-threatening mission with even half a dozen people in the CIA who did not absolutely have to know.'"

The fact that the Carter administration withheld notification for a protracted period does not, of course, justify the Reagan administration in doing so, or vice versa. But why was Reagan's case treated as a terrible offense, demanding congressional hearings, evoking fulminations about the fall of our democracy, and culminating in countless hostile books and articles? And why, when the same thing was done by Carter, was there no slightest murmur of protest?

Exactly the same double standard prevailed on the questions of trading arms for hostages and dealing directly with hostage-takers. In both of these, the Carter administration was clearly *more* culpable than the Reagan administration, but it received not even a fraction of the abuse heaped on President Reagan and his staff. That discrepancy may not tell us very much about Carter or Reagan, but it tells us a great deal about the prevailing standards of our discourse.

Ronald Reagan's Role in the Iran-Contra Affair

William E. Pemberton

The Iran-contra affair began with the Reagan administration's attempts to gain the release of hostages being held in Iran by selling arms to groups of Iranian middlemen who were thought to have influence with the terrorists. However, as William E. Pemberton explains in the following selection from his book *Exit with Honor: The Life and Presidency of Ronald Reagan*, the sale of arms to Iran was illegal under U.S. law. Furthermore, the original plan to free the hostages quickly devolved into a straight arms-for-hostages deal, with the terrorists taking more hostages to replace the ones they released, just so that they would be able to purchase more U.S. weaponry.

The other part of the Iran-contra affair involved the Reagan administration's provision of financial and military aid to the Nicaraguan contras. This assistance was in direct violation of Congress. It was supervised by Lieutenant Colonel Oliver North, who later testified that he was following Reagan's own orders to do whatever it took to help the contras. North also included funds derived from the sale of arms to Iran in his aid to the contras, thus linking the two operations.

Once all these events were made public, the complexity surrounding the two operations made it hard to discern exactly what role the president had in authorizing these illegal activities. Pemberton maintains that Reagan was directly responsible for allowing the arms-for-hostages operation to continue, and should have been aware of the nature of Oliver North's dealings with the contras.

Excerpted from William E. Pemberton, *Exit with Honor: The Life and Presidency of Ronald Reagan*. Copyright ©1997 by M.E. Sharpe, Inc. Reprinted with permission from M.E. Sharpe, Inc., Publisher, Armonk, NY 10504.

T HE IRAN-CONTRA SCANDAL, WHICH MARRED THE LAST
years of Ronald Reagan's presidency, was composed
of several separate operations. First, the United States secretly sold weapons to Iran, a terrorist state, to which such
sales were prohibited by American law. These sales violated Reagan's own highly publicized Operation Staunch, an
international campaign to stop all countries from selling
arms to Iran. Second, the United States government violated an American law, the Boland Amendment, by secretly
aiding the contra rebels in their war against the leftist Sandinista government of Nicaragua. Third, these two covert
ventures became entangled because National Security
Council (NSC) staff members, especially Lieutenant
Colonel Oliver L. North, managed both operations.
Fourth, North secretly diverted profits from the Iranian
arms sale to fund the contras.

The causes of the Iran-contra affair varied. Some Reagan advisers wanted to open relations with Iranian moderates, hoping that when the Ayatollah Ruhollah Mussaui
Khomeini died the United States would be in a position to
counter Soviet mischief making in the region. Reagan himself twisted that strategic opening into a straight arms-for-
hostages operation, counting on moderates in Tehran to
help free kidnapped Americans held by radical groups in
Lebanon. The contra part of the affair occurred because the
White House, frustrated at the restraints placed on the executive branch after the Vietnam War, wanted to counter Soviet and Cuban influence in Central America and to undermine the Sandinista government. On 1 March 1985 Reagan
said that the contras were the "moral equal of our Founding
Fathers," and on 29 April 1985 he claimed that members of
Congress who opposed contra support "really are voting to
have a totalitarian Marxist-Leninist government here in the
Americas." When Congress tried to end United States government aid to the contras, Reagan told National Security
Adviser Robert McFarlane, "I want you to do whatever you

have to do to help these people keep body and soul togeth-er." To men often forced to read Reagan's wishes by his body language, that was an emphatic, ringing order.

National Security Advisers Robert McFarlane and John Poindexter were military men, attentive to their comman-der in chief's wishes. They believed that the president had authority under the Constitution to carry out foreign pol-icy without interference from the other branches of gov-ernment, and they chafed under the restrictions imposed by Congress after the Vietnam War. The 1973 War Powers Act tried to restrict an "imperial presidency" from engag-ing in military adventurism. The 1974 Hughes-Ryan Amendment required the president to "find" that a covert action was important to national security and to report such actions to Congress in a "timely fashion." By 1981 the process required a presidential finding to be in writing and "timely" was interpreted as a few days, not months or years. Patriotic NSC staff officials, who believed that a strong president in charge of foreign affairs best served the national interest, had to interpret laws that they believed hampered the chief executive and weakened the nation.

Each of the three investigatory bodies that later exam-ined Iran-contra concluded that Ronald Reagan was mainly responsible for it. The congressional investigating commit-tee, for example, said, "If the President did not know what his National Security Advisers were doing, he should have." Independent counsel Lawrence E. Walsh concluded, "Presi-dent Reagan created the conditions which made possible the crimes committed by others by his secret deviations from announced national policy as to Iran and hostages and by his open determination to keep the contras together 'body and soul' despite a statutory ban on contra aid.". . .

The Decision to Aid the Contras

The contra part of Iran-contra began to unfold quickly in 1981. After Nicaraguan dictator Anastasio Somoza fell in

July 1979, Daniel Ortega Saavedra, who led the most ex-
treme leftists within the Sandinistas, began to consolidate
his position and push more moderate elements aside. He
established close ties to Moscow and allowed weapons to
flow from Nicaragua to rebel groups in El Salvador. That
gave the administration activists the cover they needed.
They would argue that they were not trying to overthrow
the Sandinistas but to stop the export of arms and revolution. Nicaragua posed a difficult problem for Washington,
however, because the leftist Sandinista government operat-
ed under a liberal constitution and in 1984 held democratic elections. Administration hard-liners believed that the
Sandinistas were committed communists intent on using
Nicaragua as a base to spread revolution, but moderates
and liberals believed that the young revolutionaries had
begun needed reforms in their country and that through
negotiations could be induced to stop exporting arms and
revolution to neighbors.

[Secretary of Defense Caspar W.] Weinberger, [Rea-
gan's first Secretary of State Alexander M.] Haig, [UN ambassador Jeane] Kirkpatrick, [CIA director William J.]
Casey, [Reagan's second secretary of state George P.]
Shultz, and other major figures pulled Reagan back and
forth and policymaking deadlocked. McFarlane later said
that he did not have the "guts" to stand up and tell Reagan
that he should examine the legalities of the contra operation: "To tell you the truth, probably the reason I didn't is
because if I had done that, Bill Casey, Jeane Kirkpatrick
and Cap Weinberger would have said I was some kind of a
commie." Deadlock within the administration, heated battles with Congress over Nicaraguan policy, and Reagan's
order to keep the contras together body and soul created "a
highly ambiguous legal environment," concluded the
Tower Board, which investigated the Iran-contra affair.

Reagan sat like a "remote sort of king . . . just not there,"
said Jeane Kirkpatrick, while she, Casey, [Reagan adviser

William P.] Clark, Shultz, and others engaged in savage, consuming battles over policy. Reagan did, however, make several important decisions. Based on an NSC discussion on 16 March 1981, he signed NSDD-17, authorizing nearly $20 million to build the contras into an effective guerrilla force. During a meeting with his senior advisers on 1 December 1981, Reagan decided to sign a finding to cover the secret operation, formally beginning the covert war against the Sandinistas that would kill thousands of people and cost hundreds of millions of dollars. . . .

The Boland Amendments

In the fall of 1982 the press began to uncover United States support for the contras, and members of Congress raised questions about American activities and goals. From the controversy came the first Boland Amendment, sponsored by Edward P. Boland (Dem., Mass.), which Reagan signed on 21 December 1982 after it passed the House 411 to 0. It prohibited the CIA and the Department of Defense from using any funds to overthrow the Sandinista government. The administration promptly said its goal was not to overthrow the Sandinistas but to support the contras as a way to encourage the Nicaraguan government to establish peaceful relations with its neighbors.

The NSC staff intensified covert military operations as the year ended, and Lieutenant Colonel Oliver North began to direct contra matters. North had served in Vietnam and had won a Bronze Star, Silver Star, and two Purple Hearts. His war experience had scarred him emotionally, many of his associates believed, making him cynical and contemptuous of Congress. He was an attractive, articulate, gung-ho Marine. He was a workaholic who did his assignments without asking for guidance; "the problem was, he needed it," an NSC colleague said. North exuded competence and self-confidence, but his operations often took on a Keystone Kops character. He was a self-dramatizing figure who had trouble telling the truth. Even those who realized that his stories at best exaggerated events still enjoyed listening to him. "God, the man could speak a blue haze of bullshit," a CIA official said. He loved to tell associates about his personal relationship with Reagan—"The old man loves my ass," he said—but the president later told associates he would not have known North if he had walked into the room, and office logs showed that Reagan never saw North alone, met him only four times, and spoke to him once on the telephone.

In 1984 the NSC largely took over from the CIA covert operations in Nicaragua. When North estimated that contra funding would run out in June 1984, the administration requested a $21 million supplemental appropriation. Speaker Tip O'Neill said the request was dead on arrival. It was at this point that Reagan directed the NSC staff to hold the contras together "body and soul." McFarlane passed Reagan's instructions to North and the two of them began to pursue third-country funding for the contras. In June Saudi Arabia agreed to contribute $1 million a month to the contras, upped to $2 million a month in 1985. When McFarlane told Reagan about the Saudi contributions, the president expressed satisfaction and told McFarlane to keep it secret. North also set up a network of associates to raise money from private donors. He provided private briefings for big contributors and at times arranged appearances by Reagan.

On 12 October 1984 political pressure forced an angry Reagan to sign Boland II, which tried to close loopholes in the earlier bill and prohibited the CIA from providing even nonmilitary support for the contras. Reagan did not withdraw his mandate to support the contras body and soul, and CIA director Casey told North: "Okay, you have got it all." Although Boland II seemed clearly to prohibit any government support to the contras, North and others argued that it did not apply to the NSC staff.

North brought an arms dealer, retired Air Force major general Richard V. Secord, and his partner, Albert Hakim, an Iranian-American businessman, into the contra supply operation. With the millions of dollars that North had raised from private sources, he and Secord set up "the Establishment," a miniature, private CIA that "you could pull off the shelf and use at a moment's notice." North used his network of supporters in the NSC staff, CIA, and Departments of State and Defense to help the Establishment pass military maps, intelligence, and other information to the contras. North and Secord soon had at their disposal a ship, munitions, airfields, airplanes and pilots, and sophisticated communications equipment. . . .

Reagan's Public Statements on Iran and the Contras

Then, on 5 October 1986, one of Secord's planes was shot down in Nicaragua, and the Sandinistas captured one man, Eugene Hasenfus, alive. North and Casey prepared for the operation to be exposed, and North began shredding files. On 8 October Poindexter briefed Reagan about the flight and said he did not know exactly who was involved, "but I think you should be careful about denying any U.S. role." Yet that same day Reagan publicly said about the crew, "While they're American citizens, there is no government connection with that at all." This was the first of many public misstatements that Reagan would make in the next few months.

In November 1986 while the administration was trying to finesse the contra story, the Iranian covert operation exploded into headlines. Under Shah Mohammad Reza Pahlavi, Iran had been a loyal American ally. In early 1979 the followers of the Ayatollah Khomeini overthrew the shah and as relations between the two nations spiraled downward, Iranian radicals took hostage the American embassy staff in Tehran. While Iranian fundamentalists portrayed the United States as the Great Satan, the Americans demonized the Ayatollah, equating him with Hitler. Although Washington left an arms embargo in place on Iran even after it released the hostages, other nations freely sold Tehran arms, and in 1983 Iran took the offensive in its long and bloody war with Iraq. The administration launched Operation Staunch to choke off international arms sales to Iran, and in January 1984 Shultz officially designated Iran as a sponsor of international terrorism and Reagan referred to it as "Murder Inc." On 30 June 1985, in a statement that came back to haunt him, Reagan said, "The United States gives terrorists no rewards and no guarantees. We make no concessions; we make no deals."...

The Origins of the Iranian Initiative

McFarlane was troubled in 1984. He feared that when the aged Khomeini died, there would be a succession crisis that the United States could not influence. With the United States ousted from Iran, not capable of influencing events there, he feared the Soviets could cause mischief in a region affecting American strategic interests. He looked for a way to reestablish relations with Iran.

The impetus for the White House to seek a "strategic opening" to Tehran came from outside Washington. In November 1984 Manucher Ghorbanifar met with former CIA agent Theodore G. Shackley, who reported the conversation to Washington. Ghorbanifar, an exiled Iranian businessman and arms dealer, said that he was a nationalist who feared that Iran was going to fall into Soviet hands. He said that Iranian destiny depended on the United States and that there were moderates like himself within Iran who wanted to restore good relations with Washington. He wanted, he said, to establish his "bona fides" with the moderates by arranging an arms sale to Iran and with the Americans by helping gain the release of United States citizens held hostage in Lebanon. . . .

Israeli intelligence forces believed that there were moderates within Iran and that Ghorbanifar had access to them. McFarlane and other Americans had an inordinate respect for Israeli intelligence and discounted the CIA's more pessimistic view of Ghorbanifar and his story of Iranian moderates. When in May 1985 Israeli prime minister Shimon Peres informed McFarlane that Iran had recently asked Israel to sell it arms and that Israel would make the sale if Washington agreed, the game began. . . .

It was Ronald Reagan who kept the Iranian initiative alive and who twisted McFarlane's concern for creating a strategic opening into an arms-for-hostages trade. Reagan assumed that the hostages were held in Lebanon by radical groups who looked to fundamentalist Iran for leadership. When Reagan started his trading, terrorists held five American hostages; when he left office they held eight men. As his experts had warned, trading arms to gain the release of kidnapped victims created an incentive to take more hostages. . . .

Trading Arms for Hostages

On 20 August 1985 Israel sent ninety-six TOW missiles to Iran. Ghorbanifar and his business associates handled the financing, using a Swiss bank account. No hostage was released. Instead, Iran demanded additional missiles, and on 14 September Israel sold Iran 408 more missiles. One hostage, Benjamin Weir, was released. The "strategic opening" had deteriorated into a strict arms-for-hostage transaction, and neither the Americans nor Israelis knew who in Tehran was receiving the missiles.

Officials in Tehran now realized that despite Reagan's harsh rhetoric about terrorists and Washington's holding its allies to Operation Staunch, the administration would trade hostages for arms. In October Iran proposed another trade, this time for more expensive and sophisticated Hawk missiles. McFarlane became concerned that the Americans were losing sight of the goal of making a strategic opening to Iranian moderates. . . .

In late November 1985 McFarlane resigned, and his deputy, John Poindexter, took over. Poindexter was a superbly educated graduate of Annapolis and held a doctorate in nuclear physics. In 1984 he had been offered command of the Sixth Fleet but had chosen to stay at the NSC. He was a highly disciplined, hardworking man, but he had little political skill. He seemed contemptuous of Congress and its constitutional role in foreign policy and military affairs. He was totally loyal to his commander in chief, even to the point, some investigators later concluded, of acting in his name to protect him from potentially embarrassing disclosures.

Before McFarlane left the NSC, he tried to end the Iranian operation. He told Reagan that it was not working, that they had set out to open dialogue with Iranian moderates and had ended up dealing with arms merchants. Reagan had him call a meeting of his national security team, which was held on 7 December 1985. Reagan, McFarlane, Poindexter, Donald Regan, Weinberger, Shultz, and CIA deputy director John N. McMahon attended. McFarlane traced the history of the Iranian operation and argued that it had gone astray. . . .

Reagan told his advisers that the American people would never forgive him if he passed up a chance to free hostages. The usually passive president felt so strongly about the issue that he defied his advisers. He said that he was not paying ransom to kidnappers but was rewarding a third party, Iran, which might be able to intervene with the kidnappers. At one point he said that, legalities aside, he had to take action to free the hostages. "Visiting hours are Thursday," he quipped, recognizing the possible illegal nature of the operation. . . .

The Scandal Is Exposed

In May 1986 the slipshod Iranian operation became positively bizarre. Reagan sent McFarlane, North, and several

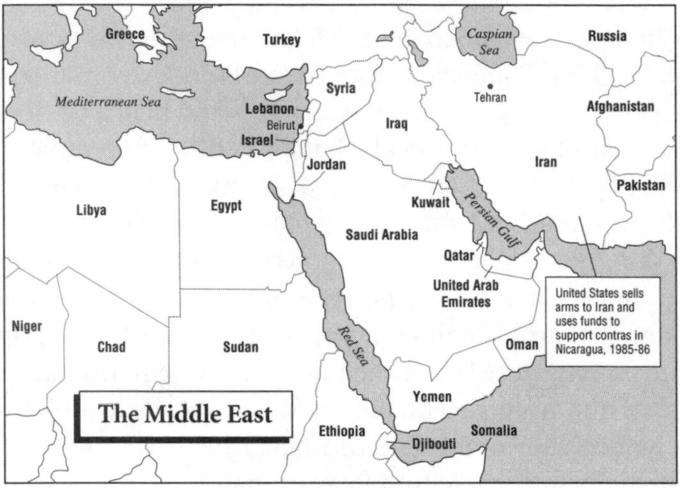
Greece
Turkey
Caspian Sea
Russia
Mediterranean Sea
Syria
Tehran
Afghanistan
Lebanon
Beirut
Iraq
Israel
Jordan
Iran
Pakistan
Libya
Egypt
Kuwait
Persian Gulf
Saudi Arabia
Qatar
United Arab Emirates
United States sells arms to Iran and uses funds to support contras in Nicaragua, 1985-86
Niger
Chad
Sudan
Red Sea
Oman
Yemen
The Middle East
Ethiopia
Djibouti
Somalia

men on a secret trip to Tehran. They used false passports, took along a chocolate cake and two pistols as gifts, and carried suicide pills to take as needed. McFarlane had expected a motorcade to meet him in Tehran to take him to a meeting with top government officials, but after they waited at the airport for awhile, Ghorbanifar arrived with several broken-down vehicles and took the party to a suite of guarded hotel rooms where they met with lower-ranking officials, obviously frightened even to be talking to the Americans. McFarlane told the Iranians to think big, to consider reestablishing good relations between their nations. He soon learned that the Iranians had little interest in a strategic opening: They wanted weapons to use in their bloody war with Iraq. It also became apparent that whatever influence they might have with the Lebanese kidnappers, they could not produce freed hostages on demand. McFarlane broke off the talks and returned to the United States. North tried to encourage the disappointed McFarlane by telling him, "It's not a total loss, at least some of the money from this deal is going to Central America." That was the first that the startled McFarlane knew of the diversion of funds.

By this time 1,508 TOW missiles, 18 Hawk missiles, and Hawk spare parts had been shipped to Iran. The Americans had also supplied the Iranians with intelligence information on the Soviet threat and on the Iran-Iraq War. The operation continued. In May and October 1986 the United States shipped additional supplies to Tehran. In July Father Jenco was released, followed by David P. Jacobsen in November. Reagan wrote in his diary, "This release of Jenco is a delayed step in a plan we've been working on for months. It gives us hope the rest of the plan will take place. We'd about given up on this." More hostages were taken, however, and when the operation ended there was one more hostage held than when Reagan began it.

There had been warnings that the Iran and the contra operations were unraveling. In October 1986 the North-Secord airplane was shot down and Eugene Hasenfus captured in Nicaragua. In mid-October Iranian students distributed leaflets describing McFarlane's visit to Tehran. On 3 November 1986 the story broke into the open when a Lebanese magazine, *Al-Shiraa,* published a description of McFarlane's activities. While one group of reporters began digging into the contra–NSC staff connection, a larger group pursued the convoluted tale of hostages and arms trades.

Many people in the Reagan White House had served under Nixon and had watched his presidency destroyed by Watergate. Some remembered that it was not the break-in that had undone Nixon but the cover-up that followed. They advised Reagan to get the whole story out quickly, admit mistakes, and assume responsibility. Reagan, however, did not believe that he had made mistakes, and, in any case, he did not feel responsible since he had always left details to his subordinates. The White House public relations people hindered matters by telling Reagan what he wanted to hear. As late as 5 December 1986 Pat Buchanan told Reagan that increasing evidence indicated that Iran-contra was an "inside-the-Beltway" [limited to Washington, D.C. insiders] story. . . .

Reagan Realizes the Full Extent of the Iran-Contra Affair

[On 21 November 1986] the president tried to end the confusion over what had happened during the Iranian operation by asking [his adviser] Ed Meese to investigate and report the facts to a meeting of senior advisers scheduled for Monday, 24 November. Poindexter, who had been present when Reagan asked Meese to make his investigation, quickly warned North, and when North saw McFarlane later that day he told him that there would be a "shredding party" that weekend.

Despite Meese's initial mistake in not sealing NSC staff records, he quickly uncovered the outlines of the story, and his rapid action perhaps saved the administration from slow disintegration. He put together a Justice Department investigating team of William Bradford Reynolds, John N. Richardson Jr., and Charles Cooper. On Saturday, 22 November, Reynolds and Richardson visited North's office to examine his records. North, who had spent the night shredding documents, was not in when the two men arrived. Reynolds found a surviving paper that indicated that money from the Iranian arms sales had been used to help the contras. Meese, shocked at the information the two men brought him, realized the dangers this diversion of funds presented to the administration. . . .

On late Monday afternoon, 24 November, Meese briefed Reagan on what he had discovered. Donald Regan said the color drained from Reagan's face and he turned pasty white. Regan believed that was the first moment that the president had heard of the diversion. A little later, Nancy found him "pale and absolutely crushed.". . .

On Tuesday, 25 November, Reagan appeared before the press, accompanied by Meese. One observer said the president "looked stricken and suddenly old." Reagan said that Meese had reported to him the results of an investigation about matters involving Iran and the contras. He now understood, he said, that he had not fully been informed about activities involving his administration. He announced his appointment of a Special Review Board to investigate the role of the NSC staff. He announced that Poindexter had resigned and North had been relieved of his duties on the NSC staff. Meese then took over. There was an audible gasp as he described the diversion.

Reagan agreed with Meese that he had to get the whole story out quickly. On 26 November 1986 the president formed the Special Review Board, chaired by former senator John Tower and including former senator Edmund S. Muskie and former national security adviser Brent Scowcroft. On 2 December Reagan asked for the appointment of an independent counsel to investigate the matter, and on 19 December a panel of judges named Lawrence E. Walsh to that position. On 4 December the House and Senate announced plans to appoint select committees to investigate the Iran-contra affair.

THE SCANDAL BREAKS

ADRIANA BOSCH

The Iran-contra affair was the worst presidential scandal since Watergate, the incident that forced Richard Nixon to resign in 1974. For Reagan, the first few months after the press first learned of the Iran-contra affair were the worst of his presidency, as Adriana Bosch describes in the following selection from her book *Reagan: An American Story*.

Initially, Reagan denied that his administration was involved in arms-for-hostages deals. When finally confronted with the evidence of the administration's dealings with terrorists and its funding for the Nicaraguan contras, Reagan claimed that the persons managing the operations, such as Lieutenant Colonel Oliver North, had exceeded their authority and not informed him of the illegal nature of the operations. However, the Tower Commission, which was appointed by Congress to investigate the affair, concluded that while Reagan was not aware of the illegal operations, it was his permissive leadership style that encouraged his subordinates to break the law, and for a time, get away with it. Faced with this censure, Reagan finally made a public apology for the Iran-contra affair.

Adriana Bosch is a filmmaker and coproducer of *Reagan: An American Story*, a 4½-hour documentary on the former president, part of the PBS series *The American Experience*. Bosch's book of the same name is a companion volume to the film documentary.

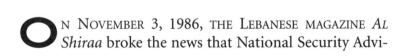

O N NOVEMBER 3, 1986, THE LEBANESE MAGAZINE *AL Shiraa* broke the news that National Security Advisor Robert McFarlane and four other Americans had visited Tehran that September. Their secret mission: to negotiate the release of hostages held by terrorists in Lebanon in exchange for weapons for Iran's military, then at war with Iraq. The Speaker of the Iranian Parliament, Ali Akbar Rafsanjani, confirmed the report the next day.

The Lebanese article marked the beginning of the scandal that would come to be known as Iran-Contra. It would shake the Reagan Administration to its foundations and reveal the deficiencies of the Reagan White House and shortcomings in the President's character.

By the time it was all over, eight defendants, including NSC staffer Colonel Oliver North and his boss, National Security Advisor John Poindexter—who had replaced Robert McFarlane—were handed convictions. Chief of Staff Donald Regan was forced to resign. CIA Director Bill Casey died of a brain tumor. Robert McFarlane attempted suicide. But perhaps the most significant casualty of Iran-Contra was Reagan's reputation. [Lou Cannon, in his book *President Reagan: The Role of a Lifetime*, writes:] "Iran-Contra forever tarnished the credibility Reagan had nurtured and preserved as an actor and politician. He would never again bask in the unquestioned trust of the American people as he had done in the red glare of Liberty Weekend."

Obsessions

Since the early months of his Administration, President Reagan had supported a Nicaraguan insurgent group—the Contras—in a covert war against the Marxist Sandinista government. Since 1984, he had also fought Congress, increasingly unwilling to fund the "Contra war."

In the Middle East, the U.S. had become the target of a terrorist campaign unleashed by Muslim extremists. Two-hundred and forty-one U.S. soldiers were killed when a truck carrying a bomb crashed through the gates of the U.S. Marine barracks in Beirut in November 1983. And

Shiite terrorists had kidnapped and continued to hold hostage seven U.S. citizens, including William Buckley, the CIA station chief in Beirut.

Keeping the Contras alive in Central America and freeing the U.S. hostages in the Middle East became obsessions for Ronald Reagan. "No problem was more frustrating to me than trying to get the American hostages home," he later wrote. "Almost every morning, at my national security briefings, I began by asking the same question: 'Any progress on the hostages?'. . . As President, as far as I was concerned, I had the duty to get those Americans home. . . . I didn't want to rest or stop exploring any possible avenue until they were home safe with their families.". . .

Selling weapons to Tehran violated an official U.S. embargo against Iran and would surely give the impression that the President was negotiating with terrorists. The operation would have to be conducted in secret. Israel, who backed Iran in the war against Iraq, would send the weapons, and the United States would replenish Israeli stocks. . . .

Between the first shipment of 100 anti-tank missiles to Iran on August 20, 1985, and the first public disclosures in *Al Shiraa* in November 1986, the Iranians received more than 1,500 missiles. Three U.S. hostages were released in exchange, and then promptly replaced by new American prisoners in what Shultz had predicted would be a "hostage bazaar."

Reagan Denies Any Wrongdoing

At first, Reagan questioned the credibility of the news story. Barraged by questions during a press conference on November 6, he pleaded: "Could I suggest an appeal to all of you in regard to this—the speculation, the commenting and all on a story that come out of the Middle East and that has no foundation?"

But on November 13, ten days after *Al Shiraa's* disclosure, Reagan went on television to explain that the shipment of weapons to Iran had been part of an effort to improve relations with that strategically important nation. But he denied that the arms had been traded for the release of hostages.

> In spite of the wildly speculative and false stories of arms for hostages and alleged ransom payments, we did not—repeat did not—trade weapons or anything else for hostages nor will we.

"Reagan had absolutely convinced himself that he was not dealing with the kidnappers," Lou Cannon told *The American Experience.*

> He had promised that he would never deal with the people who had taken the Americans hostage. He had convinced himself that he was dealing with these Iranian moderates. Reagan is a classic model of the successful child of an alcoholic: he doesn't hear things and doesn't see things that he doesn't want to hear and see. And that's the thing you learn, you learn that as a child, and Reagan learned it.

. . . The next day, a poll published by the *Los Angeles Times* showed that only 14 percent of the American people believed the President when he said that he had not traded arms for hostages. . . .

The Administration Under Siege

Reagan's greatest asset, his honesty, was in question. At a press conference on November 19, reporters, who had up to that point treated Ronald Reagan with a degree of deference, hammered him with questions.

> Helen Thomas: Mr. President, how would you assess the credibility of your own Administration in light of the prolonged deception of Congress and the public in terms

of your secret dealings with Iran, the disinformation?

Bill Plante: The record shows that every time an American hostage was released, there had been a major shipment of arms just before that. Are we all to believe that is just a coincidence?

The President dodged questions and fumbled answers. "This whole irresponsible press bilge about hostages and Iran has gotten out of hand," Reagan wrote in his diary. He was feeling under siege, and it was about to get much worse.

November 24, the Monday before Thanksgiving, Chief of Staff Donald Regan received an early morning telephone call from Attorney General Edwin Meese, who had been looking into the Iran affair. His investigation, Meese told Regan, had discovered, "things the President does not know." Meese demanded to see the President immediately.

The three men met at 11 A.M. in the Oval Office.

Meese informed the President that his investigation had revealed that the Iranians had paid $30 million for the weapons, but the U.S. government had only received $12 million. No one was sure where the other $18 million had gone. A member of the NSC staff, Lieutenant Colonel Oliver North, had admitted to Meese over the weekend that he had diverted some of those funds to the Nicaraguan Contras in ways which circumvented the law forbidding the Reagan Administration from aiding the Nicaraguan resistance.

To the men conducting the secret operation this was the "ultimate" irony, the Ayatollah Khomeini paying for the "Contra War." But to the three men meeting that morning, the diversion of funds spelled political disaster. . . .

Reagan Pleads Ignorance

The next day, the President and his Attorney General stood before an expectant press corps still preoccupied with getting Reagan to admit to the arms-for-hostages deal. Reagan began by defending the rightness of his Iran policy.

As I have stated previously, I believe our policy goals toward Iran were well founded. However, the information brought to my attention yesterday convinced me that in one aspect, implementation of that policy was seriously flawed.

Then Reagan turned the microphone over to Meese. It was then that Meese revealed the findings of the diversion of funds from the arms sales to Iran into the war chest of the Contras.

From then on, the press and the nation sought the answer to one question: What had the President known?

Reagan pleaded ignorance at the press conference. "The only person in the United States government who knew precisely about this was Lieutenant Colonel North," he said.

The next day, Reagan accepted the resignation of his National Security Advisor John Poindexter and fired NSC staffer U.S. Marine Colonel Oliver North, the "point man" in the operation. North was bitter. He thought he was doing "all he could" to implement the President's policies of keeping the Contras "alive body and soul." "I deeply believe that I had the authority of the President to do it," North later told investigators. . . .

Nearly fifteen years after Richard Nixon's darkest days, the ghost of scandal once again hovered above Washington. "This presidency is over," columnist Charles Krauthammer wrote. "1987 will be a Watergate year and the following an election year." Between the appearance of the article in *Al Shiraa* and December 1, 1986, Reagan's approval rating dropped from 67 to 46 percent. It was the sharpest drop ever recorded. . . .

Reagan appointed a commission headed by Senator John Tower to explore the details of the Iran-Contra operation. The investigation was impeded by two facts: Oliver

North had shredded most documents, and William Casey, the man most likely to know all the answers—including how much the President knew—was dying of a brain tumor. . . .

[On February 27, 1987,] the Tower Commission met with the President to discuss its findings.

"On more than one occasion," the Commission had found, "an aircraft loaded with weapons sat on a runway, awaiting word that hostages had been freed." Yet Reagan still refused to admit that he had traded arms for hostages.

The Commission found no evidence linking the President to the diversion of funds to the Contras, but it placed responsibility for that debacle squarely on his shoulders. "The President," Senator Tower reported, "clearly did not understand the nature of [the] operation, who was involved or what was happening. . . . He did not force his policies to undergo the most critical review . . . and at no time did he insist on accountability." Reagan's testimony to the Tower board had been disappointing: "I'm trying to recall events that happened eighteen months ago," he wrote in a memorandum dated February 20, "I'm afraid that I let myself be influenced by other's recollections, not my own. . . . My answer therefore and the simple truth is that I don't remember, period."

Reagan's growing disengagement from the day-to-day operations of his White House, the Commission confirmed, had created the atmosphere which made possible the diversion of funds from the sale of weapons to Iran to the Contras in Nicaragua. . . .

The Monday after the Tower Report, a new team would take over the operations of the Reagan White House. A transition team chosen by the new Chief of Staff Howard Baker would keep order over the weekend. . . .

Reagan Apologizes for the Iran-Contra Affair

One of Howard Baker's first tasks in trying to get the presidency back on track was to get Reagan to admit publicly that he had made a mistake in trading arms for hostages. . . .

On March 3, 1987, Reagan addressed the nation from the Oval Office.

> A few months ago, I told the American people I did not trade arms for hostages. My heart and my best intentions still tell me that's true, but the facts and the evidence tell me it is not. As the Tower Board reported, what began as a strategic opening to Iran deteriorated, in its implementation, into trading arms for hostages. This runs counter to my own beliefs. There are reasons why it happened, but no excuses. It was a mistake.

Overnight, Reagan's approval rating rebounded from 42 percent to 51 percent.

The Cover-Up That Worked

JOEL BRINKLEY

Shortly after the Iran-contra scandal first became public in October and November 1986, Congress formed the Tower Commission to investigate President Reagan's role in the affair. On December 19, 1986, Attorney General Edwin Meese also appointed an independent counselor, Lawrence E. Walsh, to pursue criminal charges against Lieutenant Colonel Oliver North, National Security Advisers Robert C. McFarlane and John M. Poindexter, and anyone else who may have been involved in the affair, including even Presidents Reagan and Bush. Walsh's investigation lasted seven years; he released his final report on January 18, 1994.

In the following article, written just a week after Walsh's report was released, *New York Times* columnist Joel Brinkley summarizes the report's findings. According to Walsh, Reagan had explicit knowledge of several important elements of the Iran-contra affair. Most importantly, according to both Walsh and Brinkley, Reagan was involved in the efforts to cover up the worst aspects of the scandal. Unfortunately, writes Brinkley, the cover-up worked: Reagan officials shredded evidence and refused to cooperate with investigators, and when Walsh did manage to indict a few of the people involved in the affair, President Bush pardoned them. By the time Walsh released his inflammatory report in 1994, argues Brinkley, the public no longer cared about the Iran-contra affair.

"**I**T ISN'T THE CRIME IT'S THE COVER-UP," GOES THE TRUism that has routinely been applied to political scandals since the Watergate cover-up forced President Richard M. Nixon from office two decades ago. Crimes can be forgiven. But lie about them . . . well, the American public generally won't stand for that.

No one seemed more cognizant of this than Lawrence E. Walsh, the independent prosecutor in the Iran-contra scandal. The most searing conclusion in his final report, issued last week, was that President Ronald Reagan had "knowingly participated or at least acquiesced in the efforts" of his aides to cover up the affair that had been launched to aid rebels in Nicaragua.

Facing likely impeachment, Mr. Nixon resigned when his role in the Watergate cover-up became known. But no one ever talked seriously about impeaching Mr. Reagan. One good reason, as Mr. Walsh's report made clear, was that the Iran-contra cover-up worked.

Senior officials refused to cooperate with the prosecutor. Others lied, destroyed evidence or withheld key information. As a result, Mr. Walsh said, some of the most damning evidence did not become known until long after the trail had grown cold.

But suppose that weren't so. Imagine that the Iran-contra cover-up had not worked and everything Mr. Walsh has uncovered—all the secret plotting, scheming, lies and violations of law not known to Congressional investigators in 1987—had become public back then, while Mr. Reagan still sat in the White House. Could the President have been impeached?

Possibly. After seven years of investigation, Mr. Walsh found that Mr. Reagan's conduct "fell well short of criminality which could be successfully prosecuted."

But constitutional scholars have long argued that a President need not commit a felony to be impeached. In fact as the constitutional provision on impeachment was

The Lessons of Iran-Contra

Independent counsel Lawrence E. Walsh concludes his final report on the Iran-contra affair with a call for more honest and open communication between Congress and the White House.

The Iran/contra investigation will not end the kind of abuse of power that it addressed any more than the Watergate investigation did. The criminality in both affairs did not arise primarily out of ordinary venality or greed, although some of those charged were driven by both. Instead, the crimes committed in Iran/contra were motivated by the desire of persons in high office to pursue controversial policies and goals even when the pursuit of those policies and goals was inhibited or restricted by executive orders, statutes or the constitutional system of checks and balances.

The tone in Iran/contra was set by President Reagan. He directed that the contras be supported, despite a ban on contra aid imposed on him by Congress. And

being debated more than 200 years ago, several of the framers argued that "mal-administration" should be among the impeachable offenses. With that in mind they settled on the Constitution's language, saying the President could be removed from office for "Treason, Bribery, or other high Crimes and Misdemeanors."

Those terms were meant to include "conduct not constituting indictable offenses," according to the authoritative "Analysis and Interpretation of the Constitution" published by the Congressional Research Service.

Reviewing the known facts about the Iran-contra affair solely on a legal basis, Harold R. Bruff, a constitutional expert at the George Washington University Law School,

he was willing to trade arms to Iran for the release of Americans held hostage in the Middle East, even if doing so was contrary to the nation's stated policy and possibly in violation of the law.

The lesson of Iran/contra is that if our system of government is to function properly, the branches of government must deal with one another honestly and co-operatively. When disputes arise between the Executive and Legislative branches, as they surely will, the laws that emerge from such disputes must be obeyed. When a President, even with good motive and intent, chooses to skirt the laws or to circumvent them, it is incumbent upon his subordinates to resist, not join in. Their oath and fealty are to the Constitution and the rule of law, not to the man temporarily occupying the Oval Office. Congress has the duty and the power under our system of checks and balances to ensure that the President and his Cabinet officers are faithful to their oaths.

Lawrence E. Walsh, *Iran-Contra: The Final Report.* New York: Random House, 1994.

said, "It seems to me that there is enough there that a fair-minded person could conclude" that impeachment "could have been looked into."

But the decision was political, not legal. Jim Wright, who was Speaker of the House in 1987, recalled that "there was an indisposition on the part of the leadership to have the kind of 13-ring circus that we saw brewing" when the affair first became known. "All kinds of committees were clamoring for a piece of this," he said. "There was a kind of volcanic anger brewing."

He and the Senate majority leader, Robert C. Byrd, agreed that "the last thing we needed was an impeachment outcry, a frontal assault on the President's integrity," Mr.

Wright said. "That would have doomed any chance for constructive activity in the Congress that session." And besides, he added, Mr. Reagan "only had a year or so left in his term."

The House and Senate agreed to form one Iran-contra committee so that, in theory, the rest of the Congress could go about its work. And Mr. Walsh was chosen to pursue possible criminal charges.

Now seven years later, far more is known. Mr. Reagan, as Americans now know, was worried he might get in trouble for what he and his aides were doing.

"I certainly hope none of this discussion will be made public in any way," the national security adviser, Robert C. McFarlane, told Mr. Reagan in June 1984, as they discussed soliciting third-party support for the Nicaraguan rebels during the period when Government assistance was prohibited.

According to notes of that meeting, reproduced in the Walsh report, President Reagan responded: "If such a story gets out, we'll all be hanging by our thumbs in front of the White House." During an interview with Mr. Walsh in 1992, Mr. Reagan said he "knew from the outset" that by selling arms to Iran, "he was acting in conflict with his own announced policies. He knew this activity was politically and legally questionable."

From those concerns sprang the cover-up.

In the weeks before the scandal broke in November 1986, senior White House officials crafted a demonstrably false chronology of events, and Lieut. Col. Oliver L. North shredded what investigators believe were documents that might have incriminated Mr. Reagan.

During the Congressional investigation in 1987, witnesses released selected information while withholding other notes and details. After Mr. Walsh started his investigation, George Bush steadfastly refused to talk to him, and other witnesses offered selective testimony.

Only three years later did Mr. Walsh discover that former Defense Secretary Caspar W. Weinberger, Mr. Bush and others all had kept detailed notes and diaries during their time in office—new information, Mr. Walsh said, that enabled him to indict Mr. Weinberger.

Even then, just a few weeks before Mr. Weinberger's trial was to begin, Mr. Bush pardoned Mr. Weinberger and the remaining Iran-contra defendants.

That knocked Mr. Walsh right off his feet. By the time he got back up, the investigation was essentially over. Mr. Walsh was able to show that there had been a cover-up, and that Mr. Reagan had probably known about it all along.

But by then nobody cared. The cover-up had worked.

What Mr. Walsh discovered is simply what most people assumed in 1987, though they had no proof. Would that have moved Congress to pursue impeachment? "I don't think so," Mr. Wright said. "We didn't want that kind of divisive distraction, a bloody constitutional crisis." The new information "wouldn't have changed that."

PRESIDENTS *and their* DECISIONS

CHAPTER

4

The Great Communicator

Reagan Was a Great Communicator of American Ideals

Dinesh D'Souza

In the following selection from his book *Ronald Reagan: How an Ordinary Man Became an Extraordinary Leader*, Dinesh D'Souza attributes Ronald Reagan's remarkable popularity as president to his leadership skills. D'Souza, who served as a domestic policy analyst in the Reagan White House, believes that Reagan formed a lasting bond with the American people throughout his two terms in office. In his public speeches, says the author, Reagan articulated, in clear and simple terms, great American ideals. Themes of optimism, conservatism, and anticommunism can be found in many of Reagan's speeches, but the overarching message that Reagan communicated was the importance of patriotism. Reagan has been called the Great Communicator, explains D'Souza, because of this extraordinary knack for inspirational rhetoric.

T HE IRAN-CONTRA SCANDAL WAS THE ONE CHANCE HIS enemies had to destroy his presidency, and they tried. But Reagan once again showed himself to be a political Houdini. To everyone's amazement, he wriggled out of his shackles and escaped. Not only that, but his greatest foreign policy achievements came after the Iran-contra scandal. With the signing of the Intermediate Range Nuclear Forces (INF) Treaty with Gorbachev in 1987, Reagan won

Reprinted with the permission of The Free Press, a division of Simon & Schuster, from *Ronald Reagan: How an Ordinary Man Became an Extraordinary Leader*, by Dinesh D'Souza. Copyright ©1997 by Dinesh D'Souza.

back his earlier renown and finished his second term more popular than ever.

How did he manage this feat? Partly it was his infectious good nature. However seriously Americans felt he had erred, they retained their fondness for Reagan the man. Moreover, most Americans didn't want to see another president fail. They appreciated what Reagan had done to restore America's self-confidence. As long as there was no evidence that Reagan deliberately lied about his participation in the transfer of funds to the contras, the country seemed willing to forgive the administration's blunder and move on.

The reason Reagan received the benefit of the doubt was that, over the previous decade, he had established a powerful bond of trust, affection, and intimacy with the American people. His TV addresses from the Oval Office echoed, for those old enough to remember, Franklin Roosevelt's fireside chats, in which FDR gave Americans the impression that he was speaking to them personally, confiding his views and seeking their reaction. Like Roosevelt, Reagan had the ability to reach a wide range of people in different spheres of life. "He did not sound like a politician," author Richard Reeves observed, "which made him a great politician."

A Great Speechmaker

Reagan's speeches are not heroic, like those of Lincoln, or grandiose, like those of Kennedy. Although several of his addresses are justly famous, he did not utter many unforgettable lines. His style was conversational, not oratorical. In his autobiography, *An American Life*, Reagan says that in preparing for a speech, he would picture a group of people, the kind of regular folk he grew up with, gathered in a bar or barbershop, and he would speak directly to them. His trademark as a speaker was the pause, the slow smile, the slight tilt of the head. He often began a sentence with the word *well* as in, "Well, I just don't believe . . .". He prepared his remarks for people to listen to them, not to read them in print. He used the classic techniques of rhythm, repetition, and alliteration to set his words to music.

His speeches are notable for their simplicity and clarity. He loved the telling statistic, but mostly his rhetoric focused on simple concepts and striking images. Frequently he drew on themes from the movies and popular culture, as when he challenged Congress to raise taxes, in the words of Clint Eastwood: "Go ahead—make my day." He emphasized a clear statement of basic principle and eschewed abstruse and technical argument. His rhetoric was aimed at the heart rather than the head. As one of his former aides put it, he didn't want people to react to a speech by saying, "That's an interesting idea." He wanted them to say, "Damn right!"

His speechwriters said that it was easy to draft remarks for him because his public philosophy was so consistent. Reagan had wonderfully talented writers, yet his speeches bear his own unmistakable imprint. Pat Buchanan was his White House communications director, but Reagan's rhetoric shows none of Buchanan's truculence. The president didn't give Buchanan-speeches; he gave Reagan-speeches. One of the president's writers, Peter Robinson, told me his research for a forthcoming speech on defense or tax cuts often involved reviewing Reagan's public statements on the issue going back to the 1970s. "He didn't steal from us," Robinson said. "We stole from him." Speechwriter Mari Maseng calls Reagan "the best editor I ever had." She was struck by the president's ability to inject a personal touch into otherwise formal prose and to communicate complex ideas in a straightforward way.

Simplicity and Clarity

Even as president, Reagan sometimes penned his own speeches. White House communications director David Gergen remembers that he drafted his first inaugural address on an airplane from Washington, D.C. to California "and when we examined his note pad afterward, we found that he had written it straightaway, crossing out only a handful of words." When Reagan delivered the speech in his inimitable style, it inspired continuous outbreaks of applause and a thunderous ovation at the end.

Reagan's Popularity

One indicator of presidential popularity is the Gallup Poll Organization's measurement of presidential job performance. Each week throughout Reagan's term, in a national poll, the public was asked "Do you approve of the way Ronald Reagan is handling his job as president?" The percent who answered "yes" is indicated below.

President Reagan's Public Approval Ratings

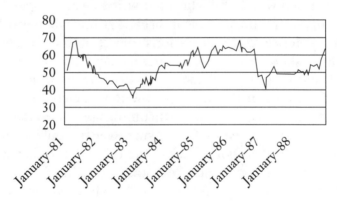

Gallup Report, December 1981–January 1989.

He also wrote many of his own best lines. The speechwriter's draft of the "Star Wars" speech said, "I call upon the nation—our men and women in uniform, our scientists and engineers, our entrepreneurs and industrial leaders, and all our citizens—to join with me in taking a bold new step forward in defense to ensure a more peaceful and stable world of the future." Reagan eliminated the bombast, focused his appeal to the scientific and technological community, and eloquently described his vision for a nuclear-free world: "I call upon the scientific community in our country, those who gave us nuclear weapons, to turn their great talents now to the cause of mankind and world peace, to give us the means of rendering these nuclear weapons impotent and obsolete."

Speechwriter Anthony Dolan's draft of the "evil empire" speech said, "Surely, those historians will find in the councils of the Marxist-Leninists, who preached the supremacy of the state, who declared its omnipotence over individual man, who predicted its eventual domination of all peoples of the earth—surely historians will see there the focus of evil in the modern world." Reagan removed the academic reference to historians, changed the past to the present tense, and clarified the moral context of the argument. In the final version, Reagan expressed the hope to his evangelical audience that the Soviet communists would abandon their ideology and "discover the joy of knowing God. But until they do, let us be aware that while they preach the supremacy of the state, declare its omnipotence over individual men, predict its eventual domination of all peoples of the earth, they are the focus of evil in the modern world."

Reagan's Patriotism

The press called him the Great Communicator, but Reagan saw himself as a communicator of great American ideals. The pundits believed he had a charmed way of saying things, but how effective would his speeches be if he were promoting yoga or Zen Buddhism? Undoubtedly the power of his rhetoric derived from both how he expressed himself and the content of his message. His critics and even some of his aides regarded his rhetoric as a symbolic device for manipulating constituencies, thus revealing a contempt for the intelligence of the American people, who were seen as easily duped or misled by Reagan's appeal to their passions and prejudices.

Reagan, however, worked hard on his speeches because he knew that a democratic leader must also be a teacher. He regarded his didactic role as one of the most important functions of a president. He had a deeper instinctive understanding of American ideals and aspirations than most people who had studied the Constitution and *The Federalist* over a lifetime. Reagan offered citizens a noble vision of a free and great country that would give meaning to their lives and allow them to realize their dreams. Ultimately he sought not just to change the laws but also to change the hearts and minds of his countrymen.

The central theme of Reagan's rhetoric was patriotism. He portrayed a vision of America as a city on a hill, a beacon to the nations of the world. "In my mind," he said, "it was a tall proud city built on rocks stronger than oceans, wind-swept, God-blessed, and teeming with people of all kinds living in harmony and peace, a city with free ports that hummed with commerce and creativity, and if there had to be city walls, the walls had doors and the doors were open to anyone with the will and the heart to get there." As these images suggest, Reagan's conception of America was inclusive. He saw the United States as a land of immigrants, where one's origins matter less than one's destination. He sought to export the American ideal to other countries in the firm conviction that it reflected global aspirations. His "American exceptionalism" was inextricably united with American universalism.

Many intellectuals take a sardonic view of such rhetoric, so it is worth asking what in Reagan's view made America such a great country. Unlike many of his critics on the left, Reagan never despised the materialistic accom-

plishments of a free society. He did not mind when Senator Howard Baker defended his policies in purely bour-
geois terms: "People can buy cars and houses and take va-
cations again." Like Tocqueville, Reagan seemed to accept
that self-interest is a necessary foundation for liberal democratic regimes.

Yet unlike many traditional conservatives, Reagan saw
no necessary conflict between self-interest and civic virtue.
He believed that people get the greatest satisfaction by
doing good for their families and communities. Reagan
was confident that if Americans were given greater political and economic freedom, they would use it productively
and decently. Freedom, in Reagan's view, promotes not just
the good life but also the life that is good. He insisted that
when we place confidence in people, we bring out the best
in them. Thus, Reagan's optimism provided a link between
his belief in freedom and his belief in virtue.

At the same time, he considered it the responsibility of
political leaders to use example and encouragement to in-
struct citizens in the highest uses of liberty. Reagan believed
that freedom creates the conditions for heroism and urged
Americans to use their freedom to perform noble deeds for
their communities and their country. This was the significance of the "hero in the balcony" that he frequently recognized in his speeches. Reagan invented that tradition.

Reagan's Heroes

Reagan's heroes were men like Lenny Skutnik, who threw
himself into the Potomac River to rescue the drowning
survivors of an airline crash, and Martin Treptow, who was
killed in action in World War I after fighting "as if the
whole struggle depended on me alone." Reagan delivered
perhaps his most moving paean to heroism in June 1984
when he addressed sixty-two Rangers on a windswept
beach in Normandy on the fortieth anniversary of their
death-defying landing: "These are the boys of Point du

Hoc. These are the men who took the cliffs." Lou Cannon reports that tough and jaded men wept when they heard Reagan's words—not just the Rangers themselves, but also Secret Service agents and American journalists.

The people Reagan held up as role models weren't Horatio Alger figures—men who started with nothing and became business tycoons. Reagan admired entrepreneurs and scientists, whom he saw as explorers crossing new frontiers of knowledge in order to expand human possibilities. But his real heroes were common folk who performed uncommon feats of self-denial and courage. Mostly he admired soldiers, firefighters, and police who place their lives in danger to preserve freedom and allow Americans to sleep safely at night. No one can reasonably argue that it is in a person's self-interest to do this. Moreover Reagan believed that human worth is tested, and greatness emerges, from the crucible of conflict.

THE MYTH OF REAGAN AS A GREAT COMMUNICATOR

WILBUR EDEL

Ronald Reagan was an extremely charismatic individual who, as president, had an extraordinary ability to influence public opinion, maintains Wilbur Edel in his book *The Reagan Presidency: An Actor's Finest Performance*. However, Edel believes that Reagan's popularity does not justify his being thought of as a great communicator. He maintains that rather than being a great leader, Reagan was popular because he told people only what they wanted to hear.

Reagan often did not fully understand the issues he discussed with reporters, Edel writes, and this led to many blunders in which the president produced facts, statistics, or anecdotes that were simply not true. Worse, Reagan would sometimes exaggerate his own ignorance of an issue or even knowingly lie to the media in order to advance his own agenda. Because Reagan propagated so much misinformation, Edel finds Reagan's nickname—the Great Communicator—highly inappropriate. Edel is professor emeritus of political science at Lehman College of the City University of New York.

IN HIS POLITICAL CAREER REAGAN WAS ANYTHING BUT ORDINARY. His ability to judge what the public wanted to hear was superior to that of his professional advisers. And his knack of getting his message across with the greatest possible impact put him on a par with Franklin D. Roosevelt and John F. Kennedy. He was especially effective on television

Excerpted from *The Reagan Presidency: An Actor's Finest Performance*, by Wilbur Edel. Copyright ©1992 by Wilbur Edel. Reprinted by permission of Hippocrene Books, Inc.

broadcasts in which he was undisturbed by inquiring reporters or other distractions. Knowing every trick in the cameraman's book, he never failed to make use of the medium that most closely resembled the controlled setting of a Hollywood studio. Even the 10- or 15-second "photo opportunities" offered by meeting with foreign dignitaries, or signing an important piece of legislation, or simply waving a smiling good-bye from a helicopter on the White House lawn, were carefully planned to allow for television coverage.

Particular care was taken with the staging of press conferences, each of which was preceded by two days of rehearsals in which answers were supplied for all the questions that the White House staff could anticipate. Even the president's entry into the press room and his position in front of the open doors, Mike Deaver later explained, was part of the effort to present the best possible picture for a television audience. Reagan's chief press spokesman for six years put the case in a single sentence: "Underlying our whole theory of disseminating information in the White House was our knowledge that the American people get their news and form their judgments based largely on what they see on television.". . .

Confusing the Facts

For all his pretense at realism, Reagan was never concerned with any facts except those that supported his preconceived notions of good and evil, truth and falsehood, the real and the make-believe. Those that did provide such support, he came to accept as true and representing reality. Having memorized them—a feat he performed as an expert—he would repeat them over and over. This became apparent to observers early in Reagan's political career. Lou Cannon put it this way:

> What unnerved reporters who spent considerable time
> with Reagan . . . was not his misstatements but his pro-

clivity for repeating the same memorized answers over and over again in the manner of a man who is saying them for the first time. It was as if someone had hit the "play" button on a tape cassette recorder.

During his governorship, the play button would produce stock answers to questions about his administrative inexperience and the support he was getting from the John Birch Society. By the time he reached the White House, the memorized messages had turned to descriptions of the Evil Empire and America's "window of vulnerability."

It may be true that Reagan regarded every memorized opinion and explanation as a fact, even though this was not always the case. His long-time friend Mike Deaver wrote about Reagan's "inability to deceive" in his 1987 memoirs: "When Reagan believes his truthfulness is being doubted, as in the case of the Iranian arms flap . . . his anger tends to rattle him . . . he finds it inconceivable that anyone would accuse him of lying." The book in which this opinion was offered was still a display item in bookstores when the Iran-Contra hearings revealed some of the deliberate falsehoods that Reagan had perpetrated. These examples came as no surprise to those who had followed his earlier career and could remember occasions during his governorship when Reagan had knowingly lied about homosexuals in his administration and about his understanding of the abortion legislation that he had reluctantly signed.

Beyond the flat falsehoods were the misrepresentations which, had they been brought to the public's attention more forcefully, and as frequently as they occurred, might have returned Mr. Reagan to what he liked to call "the ash heap of history." One astute observer, Professor James David Barber, has written at some length about the misleading picture of Reagan's governorship that, as presidential candidate, Reagan foisted upon the public—with few challenges from either reporters or opposing candidates.

Barber pointed out that Reagan's partly false and largely misleading boast of having reduced welfare rolls, increased employment, tightened abortion laws, and cut taxes and expenditures was disproved by "recorded information presented by six leading Republican legislators who had supported Reagan in his California campaigns."

Reagan's method of handling facts did not change after he reached the White House. Following his successful drive for tax reduction, which was accompanied by sharp cuts in non-defense spending, he claimed that his tax policies were "more beneficial [to] people at the lower end of the earning scale . . . than to anyone else." Two weeks later, in a relatively obscure part of its national weekly edition, the *Washington Post* pointed out that the numbers cited by Reagan were "demonstrably wrong," that a slight increase in the share of total income taxes collected from people having over $50,000 annual income reflected the enormous gains they had realized, in contrast to the increasing poverty of the lowest income earners.

Much of the misinformation dispensed by President Reagan was a product of his ignorance. Calling a special meeting of reporters to update them on plans for MX missile production, which he had discussed that very morning with Republican and Democratic members of the Senate, the president's description of a compromise agreement reached with the legislators only served to confuse his listeners. Asked what effect the agreement would have on basing modes, he went into a second lengthy explanation that led one bewildered reporter to ask, "Where is the compromise, and who was involved?" Reagan's answer was, "Well, the compromise is going to involve—would you like to explain what the compromise is, John Tower?" Senator Tower, who had been at the morning meeting, explained in one paragraph what the president had failed to explain in eight.

The most memorable of Reagan's blunders—also on his favorite subject of the military buildup—was one he later denied having made. However, the taped record of his May 14, 1982 statement contained the following bit of "reasoning" on his approach to arms reduction:

> [N]othing is excluded. But one of the reasons for going at the ballistic missile—that is the one that is the most destabilizing. . . . That is the one that people know that once that button is pushed, there is no defense; there is no recall. . . . Those that are carried in bombers, those that are carried in ships of one kind or another, or submersibles, you are dealing there with a conventional type of weapon or instrument, and those instruments can be intercepted. *They can be recalled* if there has been a miscalculation (emphasis added).

Two years later, *Washington Post* writer Philip Geyelin remembered that Reagan had made the same assertion—that missiles from submarines and airplanes "could be called back"—at a February 1982 breakfast news conference which was not reported in the *Public Papers of the Presidents*. At neither 1982 meeting was the recall statement challenged, but two months after Geyelin's article appeared, and one day after Reagan's presidential debate with Walter Mondale, reporters raised the question at the Kansas City airport. At that point Reagan said he had been talking about "submarines and airplanes, that *they* could be called back," which would have made sense, but was not what he had said on either of the two earlier occasions.

Often it is difficult to determine whether a Reagan anecdote was the product of his own imagination or if it had been told to him by a well-wisher or given him by his own staff. An example of a clearly fabricated item was included in a 1982 speech that he made in support of Texas Governor Clements. On that occasion, Reagan quoted Supreme Court Justice Oliver Wendell Holmes as saying, "Keep government poor and remain free." This quote was taken from a longer statement in Reagan's autobiography, which also credited Holmes with saying, "Strike for the jugular. Reduce taxes and spending." Holmes never said any of those things, as researcher Walter Scott pointed out just before the 1982 election. But having said it once, Reagan had the line engraved in his memory and could call it up at will. . . .

Anecdotes about the misuse of welfare funds were among Reagan's favorites. In that area he simply accepted—and passed on—any story that would illustrate the evils of welfare. Many incidents of welfare fraud were care-

Reagan's Gaffes: Honest Mistakes or Deliberate Distortions?

Reagan's habit over the years of making erroneous statements and palming them off as facts baffled many observers. Much of the fascination came from trying to decide whether Reagan's gaffes were deliberate distortions, conscious acts of deception, or simply evidence of ignorance of the subject. [Speaker of the House] Tip O'Neill adhered to the latter view. . . ."He knows less than any President I've ever known," O'Neill once said, more in sorrow than in criticism. But others took the more cynical position that Reagan purposely skewed the truth to bolster points he was trying to make. According to this view, the old actor looked upon facts in a speech much as he had lines in a movie script: that is, it was perfectly all right to make changes as long as the revisions improved a scene or strengthened the overall performance. . . .

Historical distortion became one of Reagan's specialties. In a speech he delivered in the spring of 1982, he informed his listeners, "Justice Oliver Wendell Holmes once said, 'Keep the government poor and remain free.'" A member of the White House speech-writing team later

fully documented by employees of the Health and Human Services Department, but Reagan did not stop with those. He preferred juicier items than the routine cases of multiple claims that eventually were caught by the responsible government agency. One of the many examples was his tale of an individual purchasing one orange with food stamps and using the change to buy a bottle of vodka. Apart from the fact that food stamps could not be used to buy liquor of any kind, change from a food stamp purchase may not exceed 99 cents, which would not be enough to buy even

---

revealed that the President "came up with that one himself. Holmes never said anything point-blank exactly like that." When consulted, Holmes scholars maintained that the late jurist never said anything *remotely* like that. . . .

On another occasion, in chastising other governments that had threatened to use nuclear arms to resolve their disputes, Reagan averred, "When the United States was the only country in the world possessing these awesome weapons, we did not blackmail others with threats to use them." That show of restraint would have been news to those Japanese citizens who had the misfortune of being in Hiroshima or Nagasaki in August 1945. Beyond that, both Truman and Eisenhower later threatened to use nuclear weapons during critical moments of the Korean War, at a time when, although the absolute monopoly had recently come to an end, the United States still had an effective monopoly of long-range delivery systems. In each instance, the threat may well have been justified, but it was sanctimonious to pretend that American Presidents never flaunted superior military power when it was at their disposal.

Bob Schieffer and Gary Paul Gates, *The Acting President.* New York: E.P. Dutton, 1989.

the cheapest brand of vodka. When queried about such stories, the only defense his aides could offer was that "the president was misinformed.". . .

More than any previous president, Reagan relied on his speech writers to provide not only the detailed information he refused to grapple with in his everyday administration of the nation's affairs, but the theatrics more commonly associated with Hollywood scripts. As one journalist has pointed out, the "hired word-processors" in the White House receive little of the credit that the public readily grants to movie script writers. Put pithily by Ellen Goodman:

> In politics . . . we reverse the theatrical rules. The audience assigns authorship to the person who delivers the lines, rather than to the person who writes them. We know what the president "said" today, when in fact he may only have read it today.

. . . To assert that "the Great Communicator" was not an appropriate title for Ronald Reagan is not to deny his very considerable ability to convince the public that he was the man to raise the country out of despair and on to new heights of glory. Two sweeping election victories demonstrated the effectiveness of his appeal. . . .

What kept Reagan immune from the virus of public criticism was his extraordinary ability to convince people that he was not really part of the evil thing called government, that he was in the White House not as a politician, but as a crusader intent on cleaning up the mess left by previous administrations. Representative Patricia Schroeder had named him "the Teflon president," and his most knowledgeable biographer made a similar observation when he devoted an entire newspaper column to a demonstration of how "bad news just won't stick to him." Even overseas, the power of the Reagan personality was evident, especially when he addressed non-political audiences. The

New York Times headline on a news story about his talk to students at Moscow University said it all: "President Charms Students, But Not by Dint of His Ideas."

James Reston once remarked that the American people didn't "elect" Ronald Reagan, they "fell in love with him." The extraordinary nature of his appeal is revealed in speech-writer Peggy Noonan's book *What I Saw at the Revolution*, which glows with the love for Reagan that she freely admits, even as she characterizes his mind as "barren terrain." Public opinion polls certainly support Reston's view. From 1981 to 1988 Gallup pollsters asked not only whether people approved or disapproved Reagan's policies, but whether they approved of him as a person. Only once, during the 1982 recession, when approval of his performance as president fell to a low of 37 percent, did the personal rating drop slightly below 70 percent. In the darkest days of the Iran-Contra affair, when 75 percent of the polled population believed Reagan had not told everything he knew, his personal approval rate held within a range of 71 to 74 percent. . . .

Readers concerned only with the accuracy or reliability of Reagan's statements might well wonder what earned an individual so indifferent to the facts a title like "the Great Communicator." Reagan may have expressed it best himself when, in his farewell address, he acknowledged having "won" that nickname: "I wasn't a great communicator, but I communicate great things." His explanation fell flat only when he identified the great things as the concepts that made up the Reagan Revolution. That was merely an attempt to establish as a matter of record that all his policies reflected the will of the people and the "rediscovery of our values and our common sense." If he won the title for anything, it was for frequently broadcasting—with throat-catching emotion—what the people of any nation love to hear: that they are the earth's bravest, noblest, most resourceful and generous men and women, that they are

God's chosen people, living in a country designed by the Deity to preserve all that is good and to save the world from all that is evil.

This was the essence of Reagan's appeal—wholly personal, highly emotional and, as election results so forcefully demonstrated, eminently more compelling than indications of administrative competence, intellect, or erudition. Indeed, had it not been for the Twenty-Second Amendment, which limits a president to two terms in office, Reagan might well have been given an opportunity to extend the myth of the Great Communicator from eight to twelve years.

REAGAN THE ACTOR

BOB SCHIEFFER AND GARY PAUL GATES

In their sardonically titled book *The Acting President*, excerpted below, Bob Schieffer and Gary Paul Gates, who both served as journalists with CBS News throughout the Reagan presidency, attribute Ronald Reagan's popularity as president largely to his ability to act. Pointing to the many gaffes Reagan made in his encounters with the press and with other politicians, they argue that Reagan knew little about politics: Just as he relied on having a prepared script and a director as an actor, so did he rely on speech writers and political advisers as president. In their view, the former president's acting skills also account for his success with the media, since a trained actor is always conscious of appearing his best.

O NCE HE LEFT THE MIDWEST, REAGAN'S MOVIE CAREER became the beacon that led him to everything else that followed, and when he ventured into a political career, a part of him remained firmly anchored to his Hollywood past. It provided him with a secure frame of reference in the insecure world he now found himself in, and it was the prime source of the anecdotes he was so prone to relate. He told those yarns from his movie days not only to entertain his listeners—although, for an actor, that was certainly part of it—but to draw analogies between his past and the present that, much of the time, were not altogether apt. . . .

Hollywood Anecdotes

Even after he had gone on to the White House, Reagan continued to draw on material from his Hollywood reservoir. During the period when Lebanon was in turmoil and terrorist attacks were an almost daily occurrence in Beirut, the Lebanese foreign minister visited Washington and, in a meeting with Reagan, tried to explain the intricate political factions that were rending his country. It was a complex subject, one that even the most well-informed President might have found difficult to grasp. Even so, the foreign minister was somewhat taken aback when, after he finished his briefing, Reagan cheerfully remarked. "You know, your nose looks just like Danny Thomas."

Tip O'Neill, the former Speaker of the House, has his own favorite anecdote. On Inauguration Day in 1981, Reagan went to O'Neill's office to change clothes after the swearing-in ceremony on the steps of the Capitol. While there, he couldn't help but notice a huge and ornate oak desk that seemed to take up nearly half the room, and he told the Speaker how much he admired it. O'Neill thanked the President and acknowledged that it was one of his most prized possessions. He then went on to say that the desk had quite a history because it once belonged to Grover Cleveland when he was President. To which Reagan replied: "That's very interesting. You know, I once played Grover Cleveland in the movies."

O'Neill politely corrected his visitor. "No, Mr. President, you're thinking of Grover Cleveland *Alexander*, the ball player." Reagan had indeed played the old Hall of Fame pitcher in a film called *The Winning Season* and, as fate would have it, O'Neill had recently seen it on television. As might be expected, the Speaker couldn't resist dining out on that story, and when one of his colleagues in the House heard it, he quipped that perhaps Reagan was under the impression that Grover Cleveland's schedule in the White

Polishing His Performances

It's been said that Reagan's success was based on the fact that he had been a movie star. That misses the point. His background as a film actor helped in his public appearances, of course, and, as actors do, he was careful to keep himself fit and active. On stage, he was an accomplished and guileful political performer. He was the oldest man ever elected president, but he turned his age into an advantage, using it as the source of endless, self-deprecating funny lines. In a 1984 presidential debate with Walter Mondale, he said, "I will not make age an issue in this campaign. I am not going to exploit, for political purposes, my opponent's youth and inexperience." Mondale was fifty-six, a former senator and vice president; Reagan was seventy-three. That triumphant one-liner, and many others as effective, was not accidental. Reagan took great care to polish his performances. It was said of him that he spent more of his time rewriting his speeches and public addresses than any other president. He was proud of his background in motion pictures. At the end of his second term, according to columnist George Will, "he said he sometimes wonder[ed] how presidents who have *not* been actors have been able to function."

John Chancellor, *Peril and Promise: A Commentary on America*. New York: Harper & Row, 1990.

House had been as light as his own, and that he spent his idle afternoons pitching for the old Washington Senators.

Following Directions

The congressman was referring to the laid-back management style that soon became Reagan's trademark, and that, too, can be traced to his Hollywood training. Under the system established by the major studios, movie stars—even those in the second echelon—were a pampered breed who had almost everything done for them. Their scripts were provided by writers. The glamour was furnished by the makeup staff and the wardrobe department. The lighting and sets and camera angles were the handiwork of the technical crews. Above them all was the supreme commander of the enterprise, the director, who made all the critical decisions and told the actors when to move and how to recite their lines. It was a fairly mechanical process, and some actors, accustomed to the more liberating atmosphere of the stage, found movie work frustrating to their own creativity.

Yet Ronald Reagan thrived in that stifling milieu. He had no real background in the theater and no professional training to speak of, and so he welcomed a process in which all he had to do was follow directions. There was, of course, a bit more to it than that—lines had to be memorized, proper emotions expressed—yet the actors knew that the director and his cohorts behind the cameras were united in an effort to make them look good when they appeared on the screen. This reliance on the guidance of coworkers, whose job it was to make the stars shine, carried over into Reagan's political career and helps to explain his remarkable passivity and the broad delegation of authority that puzzled so many Washington observers when he became President. . . .

Finally, there was the triumph of craft, the fine points of acting technique, that Reagan brought into politics. Back in 1937, when he made the screen test that landed him the contract with Warner Brothers, his new employers were impressed by Reagan's natural assets: his good looks, his pleasant personality, and his resonant, expressive voice. But beyond that, the young actor had a great deal to learn.

While working on one of his first movies, a veteran

cameraman, James Van Tree, taught Reagan a few basic techniques: how to react to the camera during close-ups and how to be conscious of posture and balance so that he would look as good in profile or from the rear as he did when he was directly facing the lens. Reagan later recalled the value of those early instructions in *Where's the Rest of Me?*, his 1965 prepolitical autobiography. "Very few of us," he wrote, "ever see ourselves except as we look directly at ourselves in a mirror. Thus we don't know how we look from behind, from the side, walking, standing, moving normally through a room. It's quite a jolt." But he soon learned to conquer the jolt, to be aware of how he looked at all times and from all camera angles. In recent years, several photographers noted how remarkable it was that Reagan never seemed to have been caught off guard when his picture was being taken. Even though he often appeared to be unaware that he was being photographed, there was never a slouch, an awkward gesture, an unflattering scowl, or any of the other unconscious defects that show up in candid shots of conventional politicians. The reason seems simple enough: the trained actor is always "on" when he appears before his public.

REAGAN WAS A CHARISMATIC LEADER AND A SHREWD POLITICIAN

DAVID MERVIN

In this excerpt from his book *Ronald Reagan and the American Presidency*, David Mervin takes issue with the view that Ronald Reagan was a likeable person but a poor politician. Likeability, he maintains, is an underestimated political asset, since it enables a president not only to handle the media effectively and help shape public opinion, but also to work with congressional legislators. Moreover, writes Mervin, Reagan shrewdly exploited his own charisma. Mervin rejects the idea that Reagan was an "amiable dunce": Reagan's close associates report that although he was not an intellectual person, he nevertheless possessed a photographic memory and was always able to clearly and effectively communicate his policy objectives. Mervin, a senior lecturer in politics at the University of Warwick in Great Britain and also the author of *George Bush and the Guardianship Presidency*, concludes that Reagan's political skills have been seriously undervalued by his critics.

O NE INTANGIBLE BUT IMPORTANT QUALITY THAT ROOsevelt, Eisenhower and Reagan shared was likeability, a major political resource in an anti-authority political culture where leadership is so dependent on persuasion. Like the other two, Reagan was a physically attractive man with an agreeable upbeat personality; he moved easily and comfortably on the public stage, radiating warmth and charm and generating affection among others. The absence of such personal characteristics was a considerable handicap to some otherwise highly successful American politicians. Richard Nixon was sufficiently respected to win re-election by a landslide, but likeability was not one of his strengths even before the Watergate revelations. When Lyndon Johnson queried why he was not well liked, he had to endure Dean Acheson bluntly telling him 'Well, Mr President, you are not a very likeable man.' If people had liked Johnson more, he would almost certainly have been re-elected. Similarly, if Nixon had been more likeable, Watergate might never have occurred, or the president might have survived the crisis.

Likeability Is a Political Asset

Throughout his life others have found Reagan to be an especially pleasant man. As president, both in face-to-face situations and from a distance, he came across as an unpretentious person relatively free of the pomposity and sense of self importance that afflicts most of those prominent in public life. As Garry Wills [author of *Reagan's America*] noted, 'He is endlessly likable, without the edgy temperament, the touchy pride, that drives some who become superstars.' Many critics have accused Reagan of vacuity and sloth, but few would deny him the 'nice guy' label.

Erwin Duggan in an article with the title, 'Presidential Likeability: Is Niceness Enough?' not surprisingly concluded that niceness, by itself, was not enough, but that it was an asset to Reagan in the exercise of his ceremonial duties as head of state. Reagan was, undoubtedly, especially good in the ceremonial role, but the political significance of his likeability surely extends further than that. For instance, it provides part of the explanation for his hold on American public opinion. This can be exaggerated; in fact, Reagan was not especially popular for much of his first term and

President Reagan's likeability, physical attractiveness, and considerable charisma were major political assets and contributed greatly to his popularity and successful dealings with legislators, the media, and the American public.

his standing in the polls depended on matters other than likeability, such as the state of the economy. Nevertheless, the fact that so many Americans liked Reagan personally, in many cases notwithstanding their dislike of his policies, was, in itself, one of his great political strengths.

This also helps to account for his unusually good relationship with the media—another advantage of great political consequence which Roosevelt and Eisenhower also enjoyed. Liberal commentators often expressed concern at the 'easy ride' that President Reagan was given by the print and broadcast media and alluded darkly to the machinations of image makers like Michael Deaver. No doubt these activities helped, but it was also the case that journalists, cameramen and others in the media warmed to Reagan in a way that was not the case for some other presidents. He went out of his way to be obliging and civil to those who worked in the news industry. Reagan had been a reporter himself and knew it made good political sense, but, beyond that, such behaviour came naturally to him. One source illustrates this point by reference to Reagan's habit of freely responding to questions thrown at him by reporters. The latter soon found out, 'that if they shouted a question to Reagan, loudly enough for him to hear, he was incapable of not stopping, turning and answering. . . . It seems to be an instinctive part of Reagan's personality to respond to anyone who addresses him.' Such politeness, unusual among politicians, was greatly alarming to the president's advisers, but furthered his popularity with journalists and, no doubt, influenced their presentations. Hedrick Smith, a senior figure in the White House press corps, notes:

> Sheer likability . . . has been a great asset to Ronald Reagan . . . news coverage of a public figure can be affected by the personal feelings of the press corps. Popular, likable presidents such as Eisenhower and Reagan have fared better with the press than others, such as Johnson, whom White House reporters saw as too raw and manipulative; Nixon, whom many reporters distrusted and disliked; or Carter, who was ultimately regarded as meanspirited and holier-than-thou.

Reagan's likeability was also of incalculable value in his dealings with legislators. Reagan shared with Roosevelt and Eisenhower the ability to strike up friendly and productive relations with members of Congress. If a president is to govern, he needs an effective legislative strategy and a professional legislative liaison operation is essential, but in addition there must be

> frequent use of the most precious presidential resource—the president himself. Telephone calls to wavering members, meetings with important congressional groups, intimate give-and-take sessions with important legislators and close working arrangements with congressional leaders are all necessary to maintain the broad net of relationships a president needs in Congress if he is to get anything done. A president who wishes to be

successful with Congress will be willing to commit precious personal time to persuading members and will carry out the task of persuasion eagerly and cheerfully.

There is ample evidence that Reagan was especially adept in this role. His relaxed, wisecracking, self-effacing manner put legislators at their ease and inclined them towards cooperation. 'One Roosevelt-like quality that [helped] Reagan with the modern presidential role [was] his impressive capacity to be ingratiating' a talent that few other modern presidents have possessed. Reagan did not bully and overpower representatives and senators in the manner of a Lyndon Johnson; he did not share Nixon and Carter's thinly veiled contempt for Congress, its personnel and its methods. There was no danger of Reagan humiliating or intellectually upstaging congressmen who met him in the Oval Office. 'His demeanour was one of cordiality and respect. He came across as an unassuming and agreeable man anxious to like and be liked by his visitors. Thus the president's main adversary in Congress, Tip O'Neill, found Reagan to be 'an exceptionally congenial and charming man. He's a terrific story teller, he's witty, and he's got an excellent sense of humor.'

An Amiable Dunce?

Although congressmen personally enjoyed visiting the White House during Reagan's incumbency more than a few legislators, even in his own party, were troubled by his relentlessly anecdotal style and his apparent lack of command of the detail of policy. Senator Robert Packwood, chairman of the Senate Finance Committee, complained in 1982 that, when senators expressed concern about the mounting budget deficit, the president responded with a fatuous anecdote. Similarly, Robert Michel, leader of the House Republicans, said: 'Sometimes I think, my gosh, he ought to be better posted. Where are his briefing papers?'

Reagan's preference for anecdotes over analysis, his

tendency to distance himself from the detail of policy-making and his heavy reliance on staff have all fed the suspicion that he was really not very bright. Many have concluded that he lacked the mind needed to deal with abstractions and other complexities and have shared Clark Clifford's view that Reagan was no more than an 'amiable dunce'. The *Spitting Image* caricature, some would have us believe, was not too far removed from the truth.

There is not much doubt that Reagan is not a man of exceptional intelligence in the conventional sense, but far too much has been made of his limitations in this regard. Many of those who knew Reagan in his youth and middle age clearly did not regard him as a 'dunce'. They found him a reasonably intelligent, impressively articulate and well-informed man. When he entered the White House, however, Reagan was on the verge of his seventieth birthday and doubts about his intelligence were widespread. These concerns received added weight in 1985 with the publication of David Stockman's memoirs. The portrait he painted of the president was most unflattering. Of his first encounter with Reagan during the 1980 campaign, when he was enlisted to help in the preparations for the televised presidential debates, Stockman says,

> Reagan's performance was, well, miserable. I was shocked. He couldn't fill up the time. His answers just weren't long enough. And what time he could fill, he filled with woolly platitudes. There was one question about the upcoming MBFR (Mutual and Balanced Force Reductions) conference. After a few lines he broke off, smiled, and said, 'You guys will have to forgive me now. . . . I've just lost that one completely.' You felt kind of sorry for the guy, but his lack of agility was disquieting.

Stockman decided that the president was a 'kind, gentle and sentimental' man whose 'body of knowledge is primarily impressionistic: he registers anecdotes rather than concepts'. He was an economic illiterate who could be diverted from the path of true revolution by hard luck stories and who derived his enthusiasm for supply-side theory from his personal experience of paying 90 per cent tax at the end of World War II. During the battle to secure a massive tax cut in 1981, Stockman was appalled to discover that 'the President did not have great depth of understanding about the tax code. The complexities, intricacies, and mysteries involved in the tax breaks that the Congress wanted were simply beyond him. In essence, he didn't understand the link between the federal tax structure and the budget.' In early 1984 when Stockman urged upon the president the immediate need for a major tax increase, Reagan responded with a rambling twenty-minute lecture on economic history and theory, leading Stockman to gloomily observe, 'What do you do when your President ignores all the palpable relevant facts and wanders in circles. I could not bear to watch this good and decent man go on in this embarrassing way.' Stockman's patronizing view of Reagan's intellectual limitations has very influential, but it needs to be set alongside the perceptions of other witnesses, some of whom knew the president far better.

A Balanced View of Reagan's Intellect

Donald Regan is a case in point. He was a hard-headed former businessman and as a disaffected Reaganite he is often severely critical of the president in his memoirs. Nevertheless, his overall view is far more balanced than Stockman's. Regan describes the president as 'a formidable reader and a talented conversationalist with a gift for listening'; moreover, 'his grasp of basic economic theory as it had been taught in his time was excellent, and he had kept abreast of later theory. He had no trouble understanding the leading ideas of the day, or in making reasonable judgments about the effects produced by policies based on Keynesian theory, of which he was deeply suspicious.'

Regan noted further that the president had a 'formidable gift for debate' and observed that he had seen him 'defend his ideas and critique the proposals of other heads of state with the best of them at six international economic summits.' Regan had his own doubts about the president's style of leadership, but he clearly dissents from Stockman's low view of President Reagan's intellect.

Another, even better qualified, witness who also contradicts Stockman's opinion in these matters was Martin Anderson. Over a period of seven years Anderson spent much time in Reagan's company, eventually becoming head of the Office of Policy Development and chief domestic and economic policy adviser to the president. Anderson's assessments of Reagan's intelligence must surely be taken seriously for he is no political hack; he is a conservative Republican activist, but he is also an economist and an academic of some distinction. Anderson says that Reagan, 'is highly intelligent with a photographic memory. He has a gift for absorbing great amounts of diverse information, and is capable of combining parts of that information into new, coherent packages, and then conveying his thoughts and ideas clearly and concisely in a way that is understandable to almost anyone.'

Reagan, Anderson leads us to believe, was the true architect of Reaganomics. He drew on the advice of a large number of professional economists, but, Anderson insists, 'over the years [Reagan] made all the key decisions on the economic strategies he finally embraced. He always felt comfortable with his knowledge of the field and he was in command all the way.' According to Anderson, 'Reagan did not know the latest nuances of economic theory, but he had the basics down as well as any of his economic advisers.' For more than twenty years, moreover, Reagan 'observed the American economy, read and studied the writings of some of the best economists in the world, including the giants of the free market economy—Ludwig von

Mises, Friedrich Hayek and Milton Friedman—and he spoke and wrote on the economy, going through the rigorous mental discipline of explaining his thoughts to others.' Those who persist in regarding Reagan as some sort of genial moron are obliged to find answers to the quite different perceptions of these highly qualified observers.

Temperament vs. Intellect

Ronald Reagan was much more intelligent than he sometimes appeared on the television screen or to visitors to the Oval Office. He lacked intellectual curiosity, displayed remarkably little interest in the detail of policy and had a style of leadership that was, in some respects, oddly passive. However, a high IQ, although much valued by journalists and academics, is no guarantee of success in the White House. Some extremely intelligent presidents have been failures in office, whereas Franklin Roosevelt, the most successful of modern presidents, was said to possess 'a second rate intellect, but a first class temperament'. Reagan certainly did not share Roosevelt's obsessive interest in the minutiae of policy-making, but he too had advantages of temperament. His sense of politics equalled that of Roosevelt, in marked contrast to the stridently critical and very intelligent David Stockman whose grasp of politics appears to be negligible, especially for a man who had been a member of Congress. In his book Stockman reveals his revolutionary purpose; he treated budget making as an intellectual exercise and was appalled that professional politicians did not share his grandiose ambitions. Reagan, by contrast, was a political realist rather than a utopian. The president also had a healthy belief in the division of political labour; he had himself established the broad framework of economic policy whereas it was the duty of Stockman and others to work out the details. After that had been done the chief executive was primarily responsible for selling the resultant product to Congress and the public.

Reagan's Popularity Before and After the Assassination Attempt

Haynes Johnson

On March 30, 1981, approximately two months after taking office, Ronald Reagan was shot by John W. Hinckley Jr. As Pulitzer Prize–winning journalist Haynes Johnson explains in the following excerpt from his book *Sleepwalking Through History: America in the Reagan Years*, the televised shooting threatened to seriously demoralize a nation which was still recovering from the assassination of John F. Kennedy in 1963. Fortunately, Reagan survived his injuries, and in the end the ordeal—and Reagan's graceful handling of it—greatly contributed to the enormous popularity that the president enjoyed for the next several years.

I T WAS NOT AT ALL CLEAR THAT THE AMERICANS WHO ELECT-
ed [Ronald Reagan] supported the kinds of fundamental changes he proposed. On the contrary, the evidence suggested otherwise. At that point there was nothing to indicate that a majority of Americans agreed with his ideological pronouncements. One month after he took office, a CBS/*New York Times* poll found that the public favored a balanced budget over more military spending. It opposed large tax cuts. It opposed cuts in Social Security, mass transit, pollution control, and aid to students.

Excerpted from *Sleepwalking Through History: America in the Reagan Years*, by Haynes Johnson. Copyright ©1991 by Haynes Johnson. Used by permission of W.W. Norton & Company, Inc.

Similarly, a Gallup poll taken after the election found that the American public and the president did not agree on two key campaign issues, the Equal Rights Amendment and abortion. While Reagan opposed the ERA, the public favored it by an overwhelming two to one margin. Reagan favored a ban on abortions except when the life of the mother was at stake; the public took the opposite view. It strongly was against banning any abortions. Gallup also found that a large majority differed from Reagan's views on other public questions: It wanted stricter handgun controls and favored keeping the fifty-five-mile-per-hour national speed limit; by a narrower margin, the public opposed construction of more nuclear plants. In all these, and in others, the public was not then supportive of Reagan's views and approaches.

Later it was claimed by some of his critics that he had misled the nation by hiding the nature of the changes he proposed. Or, in a corollary argument, it was charged that the press failed to do its job and disclose the severity of the changes he sought or explain their potential impact on people.

Part of the reason for the subsequent search for scapegoats was attributable to David Stockman [then director of the Office of Budget Management and an early advocate of Reagan's economic plan]. Later Stockman admitted that he and Reagan officials had deliberately kept hidden from Congress, press, and public their knowledge that the Reagan economic plan could never work as advertised and their belief that when forced to make difficult budget choices between defense and domestic spending, Congress would have to choose military over social needs. Part was attributable to the stunning success Reagan achieved, in contrast with his immediate predecessors, in securing passage of his political agenda. Still, while some duplicity was surely involved, neither Reagan nor the press was guilty of the larger charges of a deliberate conspiracy to deceive the public. As those page one headlines culled from the first weeks of his administration demonstrate, the Reagan proposals were fully and immediately aired; they formed the material for instant public debate. Reagan had practiced no deceit, nor was there any hidden agenda on his part. Americans had every opportunity to become fully informed about the scope of the political revolution being proposed.

The Assassination Attempt

Two months into his term there existed a clear and growing conflict between public desires and presidential wishes. Reagan had clearly defined his interpretation of his mandate. He had plunged ahead aggressively in an effort to turn back the political clock, but there was no assurance he would succeed and considerable reason to believe he might fail. His proposals were already stirring intense controversy, with the promise of more to come. Then, suddenly, all equations, political and personal, were altered with the as-

The assassination attempt on President Ronald Reagan was captured live on television and was replayed over and over for a horrified and anxious nation. Reagan's courage and humor during his recovery had a powerful effect on the American public.

sassination attempt on March 30, 1981, in Washington, sixty-nine days after he became president.

The attempt on Ronald Reagan's life followed a familiar pattern. Once again the would-be assassin was a pathetically disturbed young man acting out a fantasy formed by the illusory world of Hollywood, in his case repeatedly watching the film *Taxi Driver* and becoming fixated on its young actress, Jodie Foster. John W. Hinckley, Jr., was a familiar type in other respects. He was a child of wealth and privilege who became one of the nation's lonely drifters, living in a constant state of illusions as he wandered from place to place, until he sought to "prove" his love for Foster by killing the most famous person in the world. The Devastator bullets containing explosive tips that he fired from an easily purchased, cheap handgun marked the fourth time in less than twenty years that gunshots had been fired at a president of the United States from streets of a large American city.

Moments after the crackle of gunfire echoed off the stone wall outside the Washington Hilton Hotel shortly after two-thirty in the afternoon on a sodden spring day, an eyewitness said, "I knew it was more than just firecrackers." Within minutes Americans everywhere knew it had happened again: another president shot, another political promise interrupted by violence. For hour after hour that day there was no way for Americans to escape the replaying of an old national horror. Over and over, from daylight into dark, in slow motion, in stop action, and in all the other techniques of electronic communications, television brought home the latest installment of an all-too-familiar American tragedy. The sudden pap-pap of gunfire, the bodies hurtling to the ground, the hoarse shouts, the presidential limousine speeding off to the hospital emergency room, the gathering of the silent crowds standing outside in a driving rain, the ominous news bulletins reporting on the president's condition coming furiously throughout the day, the clusters of people gathered before their TV sets all forced people once again to think the unthinkable.

Reagan Handles the Crisis with Aplomb

Those television scenes formed inseparable parts of an unending spasm of violence that had struck the nation with blow after blow. For a generation, violent acts had disrupted the political process, torn at the nation's leadership, left citizens numbed by a cycle of terror.

No one could say with certainty what the cumulative impact of these acts had been on individual Americans or on the country as a whole. Obviously it had been great, and made more so by the age of instant video communications. As Americans once more sat before their television sets anxiously awaiting news bulletins and wondering what was happening to their country, this time there was a different ending. Reagan survived, and did so in a manner that won American hearts.

The bullet had entered his body below the left armpit, struck the seventh rib, glanced off the bone, punctured the lung, and lodged near his heart. Despite repeated reassurances given then and later by officials that the wound was not serious—"not all that serious," as one newspaper report typically put it—he had been gravely injured. His blood pressure was alarmingly low, his left pleural cavity was filling with blood, he was laboring for breath, and he was approaching a state of incipient shock as he was placed inside a trauma unit at George Washington University Hospital.

He displayed genuine courage and humor in adversity. When he saw the panic-stricken look on his wife's face as she watched the doctors begin examining him, he quipped: "Honey, I forgot to duck."

In a time when so many direct quotations said to have been spoken by a president and put out publicly in his name were false, to anyone who knew anything about Ronald Reagan this one was authentic. They were the identical words Jack Dempsey had spoken into the radio microphones after losing his heavyweight crown to Gene Tunney in the twenties. Reagan, the sports buff, radio fan, and budding sports announcer, must have heard them as a college student and remembered. Similarly, his joking remark to the doctors who were about to operate on him—"I hope you're all Republicans"—had the ring of the authentic Reagan.

A New Phase of Public Popularity

These remarks, when instantly relayed to the press, understandably had a powerful and positive effect on the American public. The subsequent cheerfulness and grace Reagan displayed during his long recovery in the hospital and White House, his ritual waves and smiles given during the daily long-range photo opportunities, also contributed strongly in reassuring the public. They all conveyed a sense to the public that Reagan possessed larger-than-life qualities. That his recovery itself was a far more difficult process than let on by his political and public relations advisers was not in itself significant. Reagan's survival alone was proof enough that the country's luck had turned for the better.

Reagan had entered a new phase of public popularity and acceptance; his political team effectively capitalized on them. As pollsters reported a wave of admiration for Reagan from around the country, White House officials moved to push for passage of the president's legislative program.

Typical of the media blitz instituted out of the White House was the appearance of Treasury Secretary Donald T. Regan on ABC's "Good Morning America" television program the day after the shooting. The president's temporary incapacitation, Regan said, had made his cabinet members "determined, even more, to push his program and 'win one for the Gipper.'" Similar remarks were made by the rest of the Reagan team. "We have to formulate another political campaign in which we're selling a product, not a candidate," said Reagan's closest friend in Congress, Senator Paul Laxalt of Nevada, in describing the political strategy Republicans would employ to gain passage of Reagan's tax cuts, defense increases, and domestic spending reductions.

Others immediately foresaw that the assassination attempt could have lasting political implications. Robert Teeter, a leading Republican pollster who later became a chief adviser to George Bush in the 1988 presidential campaign, shrewdly summed up what he correctly understood to be the new political realities. "It certainly makes people feel more personally sympathetic to him," Teeter told David S. Broder of the *Washington Post* hours after the assassination attempt, "and makes it harder for the Democrats to criticize him directly. A lot of his support was soft and the fact that he handled his first crisis well . . . will firm up that support. I think at the minimum it buys him more time and makes opposition harder."

A Long-Term Plus

Leading Democrats and Reagan opponents shared the sense that something of great political importance had happened. Comments of two other politicians whom Broder interviewed immediately after the shooting reflected that feeling. "I think he will remain popular throughout his term now, whether or not his program works," said William R. Hamilton, who took political polls for many Democratic members of Congress. "When he showed the ability to go through this with a quip, it was something the average man can understand. It probably makes him immune from ever dropping to the low level of personal popularity Carter reached." Morris Udall of Arizona, one of the most respected Democratic members of Congress, who himself had sought the presidency in 1976, said: "This is a long-term plus for Reagan. He has been through the fire and escaped.

There is an aura there that wasn't there before."

Within three months, as Democrats broke ranks by the scores, Congress overwhelmingly voted for the Reagan tax cuts and the big defense buildup. Reagan then stood, like Roosevelt before him, as king of Congress and legislative master of all he surveyed.

THE FIRST TRUE
TELEVISION PRESIDENT

MARY E. STUCKEY

Reagan was the first president to fully grasp the power of television in shaping public opinion, and that is why he has been variously hailed as the Great Communicator and the "Teflon President." That is the thesis of Mary E. Stuckey in the chapter devoted to Reagan in her book *The President as Interpreter-in-Chief*. As a former actor, she writes, Reagan understood the importance of mass media, and he and his advisers did their best to take advantage of this. Reagan and his administration designed press conferences for full dramatic effect: They chose what questions the president would answer, and when criticized Reagan would accuse the media of having a liberal bias. Stuckey also argues that the Reagan administration designed speeches to be simple and clear so they would fit the television news format, which favors short sound bites. Stuckey is an associate professor of communications and political science at Georgia State University.

RONALD REAGAN, THE GREAT COMMUNICATOR, THE Teflon President, is as well known for his effectiveness as a communicator as for the substance of what he communicated. More than any other modern political actor, Reagan understood the importance of mass-media communication. He understood how media work, how to use that to his advantage, and how to structure his appeals to communicate best through television, the dominant medium. As one analyst notes, "Ronald Reagan is our first true television president. His persona, messages, and behavior fit the medium's requirements in terms of form, content, and industry demands. Reagan made television the instrument of governing. His presidency provides the blueprint for public esteem and popularity."

Handling the Press

Reagan, and his staff, understood that much of politics is theater, and they designed a presidency capable of taking full advantage of that understanding. This involved both relations with the media and appeals designed for the public. In dealing with the media, Reagan and his people understood that the national media corps, despite its reputation for aggression, is in reality "fundamentally passive." Reagan understood that if he timed events in a certain way, then he could force coverage or cripple it, depending on his own agenda. Unlike either Ford or Carter, Reagan did not play into the requirements of the media; he forced the media requirements to play into his agenda, and thus maintained control. This was possible because of the central role the presidency has come to play. Television reporters rely on the president to provide news. The news the president chooses to supply can be, and all too often is, orchestrated with attention to the requirements of television, not the requirements of governance.

Reagan often blamed the media for bad news and publicly styled them as tools of the liberal opposition. In 1985, for example, Reagan said, "I sometimes feel that the journalists who cover our everyday political affairs here in Washington have a tendency to miss the real news," thus undermining the quality of what the media do report. "I've noticed that there's never a 'good news' economic story on the evening news that was not accompanied by, or buried by, finding some individuals who have not yet benefited by the economic recovery.". . .

This was a particularly strong dynamic when the media encountered a president as publicly popular and amiable as Ronald Reagan. In challenging him, the media ran the risk of being perceived by the public as hounding the president in an undignified manner, instead of pursuing presidential accountability. This was a problem the Reagan administration did its best to magnify. Reagan was very aware of the importance of staging, and of how to manage it to maximize his interests and minimize those of the press. The press was kept at a distance from the president, forcing them to yell questions as he passed, sometimes over the sound of a helicopter rotor. In addition, news conferences were rare and were used for calculated effect. . . .

Television Encourages Simplicity

"Because the Reagan administration understood [the] pattern of reportorial coverage, they took steps that influenced what appeared as news." They understood the importance of providing good visuals, usable copy, and always remembered that "television thrives on simplicity.". . .

Reagan's narrative line nearly always involved clear choices between two opposite alternatives. "This year, New Jersey is being offered a clear-cut choice between those who think government spending and taxing are the solution to our problems and those, like Tom [Kean, Republican gubernatorial candidate], who understand that government spending and taxation are the problem." These clear choices between a well-defined good and an equally well-defined evil make matters simple, easy to understand, easy to get emotional about, and easy to remember. That reality may not be so clear-cut is not material: Ford and Carter tried to use television to portray a complex reality, with little success. Reagan's speech, however unrealistic, worked well on television.

Reagan's personal style fits in beautifully with the simplicity encouraged by television. His approach to communication has always been through narrative, and his speeches are peppered with anecdotes. Two prominent scholars explain, "As all great communicators have always known, the story is probably the best way to get a point across to a wide audience and to insure that the point then sticks in people's minds." The problem with such almost exclusive reliance on storytelling as a communicative device is that it distorts reality. Real-world events do not always follow a single narrative line. Communication that forces events into such a line, regardless of appropriateness, is, if not a lie, then a distortion of the truth. . . .

Speeches and Soundbites

The role of the writer is . . . different in the new era of televised politics. Writing is increasingly more of a technical trade than a creative one: Writers search for the perfect soundbite, the perfect slogan, the perfect snappy remark that will make the nightly news and get the message across. What this misses is that communication in advertising slogans is not informational:

> Great speeches have always had great soundbites. The problem now is that the young technicians who put together speeches are paying attention only to the soundbite, not to the text as a whole, not realizing that all great soundbites happen by accident, which is to say all great soundbites are yielded up inevitably, as part of the natural expression of the text. They are part of the tapestry, they aren't a little flower somebody sewed on.

When a speech becomes nothing more than the hanger for a soundbite, then the bulk of the text is rendered largely irrelevant. The earlier, equally oral colonial period relied on slow, careful construction of an argument, built on explicit historical and philosophical premises. In today's oral and visual culture, assertion replaces argumentation, and the premises are left out entirely.

Reagan's consistency in reflecting the nation's values in his speeches and his ability to maintain composure on television aided him in becoming an effective television politician.

This is a serious problem. Public speech, in our day as well as in the colonial period, functions to express our commonality; to constitute the community. When arguments are reduced to generalized assertions, when the historical and philosophical postulates are ignored, it is unclear what exactly that sense of commonality and community is based on. Reagan's solution to this problem was to base nearly all his arguments on shared American values.

Reagan used these values as a means of inclusion, rhetorically making the audience part of the shared American value system. His use of values had the added advantage of excluding his opposition. Reagan excelled at using values as a basis for inclusive rhetoric: "No, you represent a cross section of Americans from all backgrounds, different regions across the country. In fact, you remind me very much of that one special interest group that I mentioned on Inauguration Day—the one special interest group that has been neglected and needs help—that is, we the people."

These values have strong optimistic overtones: "Perhaps because we control our own destiny, we believe deep down inside that working together we can make each year better than the old." The optimism is important, for not only does it make for easier listening, it is also better television, which tends to encourage "good, positive, upbeat pictures." Reagan's words reinforced the visual images and strengthened the overall impression of control, comfort, and security.

As far as exclusion goes, Reagan characterized his opposition as politically motivated, selfish, and self-interested, as people who loved obscure, complex theories and programs:

> The plan I outlined will stop runaway inflation and revitalize our economy, and there's nothing but politics-as-usual standing in the way of lower inflation, increased productivity and a return to prosperity. Our program for economic recovery does not rely upon complex theories or elaborate Government programs. Instead it recognizes basic economic facts of life and, as humanely as possible, it will move America back toward economic sanity.

Like television, Reagan thrived on simplicity.

APPENDIX

Excerpts from Original Documents

Document 1: A Time for Choosing

Ronald Reagan gave some of his most memorable speeches during the 1964 presidential campaign, in which he served as cochairman of Californians for Barry Goldwater. The speech he gave on October 27 of that year has since been named "A Time for Choosing" or simply "The Speech" by his admirers. In it, he spoke of many of the same themes he had in his appearances as a spokesman for General Electric: the importance of individual freedom, the dangers of big government, and the importance of lowering taxes.

I am going to talk of controversial things. I make no apology for this. . . .

The Founding Fathers knew a government can't control the economy without controlling people. And they knew when a government sets out to do that, it must use force and coercion to achieve its purpose. So we have come to a time for choosing.

Public servants say, always with the best of intentions, "What greater service we could render if only we had a little more money and a little more power." But the truth is that outside of its legitimate function, government does nothing as well or as economically as the private sector. . . .

We are for a provision that destitution should not follow unemployment by reason of old age, and to that end we have accepted Social Security as a step toward meeting the problem. However, we are against those entrusted with this program when they practice deception regarding its fiscal shortcomings, when they charge that any criticism of the program means that we want to end payments. . . .

We need true tax reform that will at least make a start toward restoring for our children the American Dream that wealth is denied to no one, that each individual has the right to fly as high as his strength and ability will take him. . . . But we can not have such reform while our tax policy is engineered by people who view the tax as a means of achieving changes in our social structure. . . .

Have we the courage and the will to face up to the immorality and discrimination of the progressive tax, and demand a return to traditional proportionate taxation? . . . Today in our country the tax collector's share is 37 cents of every dollar earned. Freedom has never been so fragile, so close to slipping from our grasp.

Are you willing to spend time studying the issues, making yourself aware, and then conveying that information to family and friends? Will you resist the temptation to get a government handout for your community? Realize that the doctor's fight against socialized medicine is your fight. We can't socialize the doctors without socializing the patients. Recognize that government invasion of public power is eventually an assault upon your own business. If some among you fear taking a stand because you are afraid of reprisals from customers, clients, or even government, recognize that you are just feeding the crocodile hoping he'll eat you last.

If all of this seems like a great deal of trouble, think what's at stake. We are faced with the most evil enemy mankind has known in his long climb from the swamp to the stars. There can be no security anywhere in the free world if there is no fiscal and economic stability within the United States. Those who ask us to trade our freedom for the soup kitchen of the welfare state are architects of a policy of accommodation.

They say the world has become too complex for simple answers. They are wrong. There are no easy answers, but there are simple answers. We must have the courage to do what we know is morally right. Winston Churchill said that "the destiny of man is not measured by material computation. When great forces are on the move in the world, we learn we are spirits—not animals." And he said, "There is something going on in time and space, and beyond time and space, which, whether we like it or not, spells duty."

You and I have a rendezvous with destiny. We will preserve for our children this, the last best hope of man on earth, or we will sentence them to take the first step into a thousand years of darkness. If we fail, at least let our children and our children's children say of us we justified our brief moment here. We did all that could be done.

Ronald Reagan, "A Time for Choosing," October 27, 1964.

Document 2: Reagan's First Inaugural Address

In his first inaugural address, given on January 20, 1981, Reagan outlined his view that many of the nation's social and economic problems could be solved by limiting the power of the federal government.

The business of our nation goes forward. These United States are confronted with an economic affliction of great proportions. We suffer from the longest and one of the worst sustained inflations in our national history. It distorts our economic decisions, penalizes thrift, and crushes the struggling young and the fixed-income elderly alike. It threatens to shatter the lives of millions of our people.

Idle industries have cast workers into unemployment, causing human misery and personal indignity. Those who do work are denied a fair return for their labor by a tax system which penalizes successful achievement and keeps us from maintaining full productivity. . . .

The economic ills we suffer have come upon us over several decades. They will not go away in days, weeks, or months, but they will go away. They will go away because we, as Americans, have the capacity now, as we have had in the past, to do whatever needs to be done to preserve this last and greatest bastion of freedom.

In this present crisis, government is not the solution to our problem. . . .

We are a nation that has a government—not the other way around. And this makes us special among the nations of the Earth. Our Government has no power except that granted it by the people. It is time to check and reverse the growth of government which shows signs of having grown beyond the consent of the governed.

It is my intention to curb the size and influence of the Federal establishment and to demand recognition of the distinction between the powers granted to the Federal Government and those reserved to the States or to the people. All of us need to be reminded that the Federal Government did not create the States; the States created the Federal Government.

Now, so there will be no misunderstanding, it is not my intention to do away with government. It is, rather, to make it work—work with us, not over us; to stand by our side, not ride on our back. Government can and must provide opportunity, not smother it; foster productivity, not stifle it.

Ronald Reagan, "First Inaugural Address," January 20, 1981.

Document 3: The Program for Economic Recovery

Shortly after he took office, Reagan gave a televised address from the Oval Office in which he outlined the economic problems facing the nation and explained his administration's plans to solve them.

Good evening.

I'm speaking to you tonight to give you a report on the state of our nation's economy. I regret to say that we're in the worst economic mess since the Great Depression. . . .

The federal budget is out of control, and we face runaway deficits of almost $80 billion for this budget year that ends September 30th. That deficit is larger than the entire federal budget in 1957, and so is the almost $80 billion we will pay in interest this year on the national debt.

Twenty years ago, in 1960, our federal government payroll was less than $13 billion. Today it is 75 billion. During these twenty years our population has only increased by 23.3 percent. The federal budget has gone up 528 percent.

Now, we've just had two years of back-to-back double-digit inflation—13.3 percent in 1979. 12.4 percent last year. The last time this happened was in World War I.

In 1960 mortgage interest rates averaged about 6 percent. They're two and a half times as high now, 15.4 percent.

The percentage of your earnings the federal government took in taxes in 1960 has almost doubled.

And finally there are 7 million Americans caught up in the personal indignity and human tragedy of unemployment. If they stood in a line, allowing three feet for each person, the line would reach from the coast of Maine to California. . . .

I'm sure you're getting the idea that the audit presented to me found government policies of the last few decades responsible for our economic troubles. We forgot or just overlooked the fact that government—any government—has a built-in tendency to grow. Now, we all had a hand in looking to government for benefits as if government had some source of revenue other than our earnings. . . .

Some government programs seemed so worthwhile that borrowing to fund them didn't bother us. By 1960 our national debt stood at $284 billion. Congress in 1971 decided to put a ceiling of $400 billion on our ability to borrow. Today the debt is $934 billion. So-called temporary increases or extensions in the debt ceiling have been allowed twenty-one times in these ten years, and now I've been forced to ask for another increase in the debt ceiling or the government will be unable to function past the middle of February—and I've only been here sixteen days. Before we reach the day when we can reduce the debt ceiling, we may in spite of our best efforts see a national debt in excess of a trillion dollars. Now, this is a figure that's literally beyond our comprehension.

We know now that inflation results from all that deficit spending. . . .

Over the past decades we've talked of curtailing government spending so that we can then lower the tax burden. Sometimes we've even taken a run at doing that. But there were always those who told us that taxes couldn't be cut until spending was reduced. Well, you know, we can lecture our children about extravagance until we run out of voice and breath. Or we can cure their extravagance by simply reducing their allowance. . . .

I've already placed a freeze on hiring replacements for those who retire or leave government service. I've ordered a cut in government travel, the number of consultants to the government, and the buying of office equipment and other items. I've put a freeze on pending regulations and set up a task force under Vice President Bush to review regulations with an eye toward getting rid of as many as possible. . . .

On February 18th, I will present in detail an economic program to Congress embodying the features I've just stated. It will propose budget cuts in virtually every department of government. It is my belief that these actual budget cuts will only be part of the savings. As our cabinet secretaries take charge of their departments, they will search out areas of waste, extravagance, and costly overhead which could yield additional and substantial reductions.

Now, at the same time we're doing this, we must go forward with a tax relief package. I shall ask for a 10-percent reduction across the board in personal income tax rates for each of the next three years. Proposals will also be submitted for accelerated depreciation allowances for business to provide necessary capital so as to create jobs. . . .

Our spending cuts will not be at the expense of the truly needy. We will, however, seek to eliminate benefits to those who are not really qualified by reason of need. . . .

Our basic system is sound. We can, with compassion, continue to meet our responsibility to those who, through no fault of their own, need our help. We can meet fully the other legitimate responsibilities of government. We cannot continue any longer our wasteful ways at the expense of the workers of this land or of our children.

Since 1960 our government has spent $5.1 trillion. Our debt has grown by $648 billion. Prices have exploded by 178 percent. How much better off are we for all that? Well, we all know we're very much worse off. When we measure how harshly these years of inflation, lower productivity, and uncontrolled government growth have affected our lives, we know we must act and act now. We must not be timid. We will restore the freedom of all men and women to excel and to create. We will unleash the energy and genius of the American people, traits which have never failed us.

Ronald Reagan, "Address to the Nation on the Economy," February 5, 1981.

Document 4: The "Evil Empire" Speech

The following excerpts are from Reagan's March 8, 1983, remarks at the annual convention of the National Association of Evangelicals. In the portion excerpted here, Reagan describes the nuclear freeze movement as well-meaning but misguided. He argues that a show of strength is neces-sary to prevent aggression from the Soviet Union, which he famously called an "evil empire."

During my first press conference as president, in answer to a direct question, I pointed out that, as good Marxist-Leninists, the Soviet leaders have openly and publicly declared that the only morality they recognize is that which will further their cause, which is world revolu-tion. I think I should point out I was only quoting Lenin, their guid-ing spirit, who said in 1920 that they repudiate all morality that pro-ceeds from supernatural ideas—that's their name for religion—or ideas that are outside class conceptions. Morality is entirely subordi-nate to the interests of class war. And everything is moral that is nec-essary for the annihilation of the old, exploiting social order and for uniting the proletariat.

Well, I think the refusal of many influential people to accept this el-ementary fact of Soviet doctrine illustrates a historical reluctance to see totalitarian powers for what they are. We saw this phenomenon in the 1930s. We see it too often today.

This doesn't mean we should isolate ourselves and refuse to seek an understanding with them. I intend to do everything I can to persuade them of our peaceful intent, to remind them that it was the West that refused to use its nuclear monopoly in the forties and fifties for terri-torial gain and which now proposes a 50-percent cut in strategic bal-listic missiles and the elimination of an entire class of land-based, intermediate-range nuclear missiles.

At the same time, however, they must be made to understand we will never compromise our principles and standards. We will never give away our freedom. We will never abandon our belief in God. And we will never stop searching for a genuine peace. But we can assure none of these things America stands for through the so-called nuclear freeze solutions proposed by some.

The truth is that a freeze now would be a very dangerous fraud, for that is merely the illusion of peace. The reality is that we must find peace through strength.

I would agree to a freeze if only we could freeze the Soviets' global desires. A freeze at current levels of weapons would remove any incentive for the Soviets to negotiate seriously in Geneva and virtually end our chances to achieve the major arms reductions which we have proposed. Instead, they would achieve their objectives through the freeze.

A freeze would reward the Soviet Union for its enormous and unparalleled military buildup. It would prevent the essential and long overdue modernization of United States and allied defenses and would leave our aging forces increasingly vulnerable. And an honest freeze would require extensive prior negotiations on the systems and numbers to be limited and on the measures to ensure effective verification and compliance. And the kind of a freeze that has been suggested would be virtually impossible to verify. Such a major effort would divert us completely from our current negotiations on achieving substantial reductions. . . .

Let us pray for the salvation of all of those who live in that totalitarian darkness—pray they will discover the joy of knowing God. But until they do, let us be aware that while they preach the supremacy of the state, declare its omnipotence over individual man, and predict its eventual domination of all peoples on the earth, they are the focus of evil in the modern world. . . .

So, in your discussions of the nuclear freeze proposals, I urge you to beware the temptation of pride—the temptation of blithely declaring yourselves above it all and label both sides equally at fault, to ignore the facts of history and the aggressive impulses of an evil empire, to simply call the arms race a giant misunderstanding and thereby remove yourself from the struggle between right and wrong and good and evil.

Ronald Reagan, "Remarks at the Annual Convention of the National Association of Evangelicals," March 8, 1983.

Document 5: Peace and National Security

Almost immediately after he entered office, Reagan began battling with Congress over his proposed increases in the defense budget. On March 23, 1983, in a nationally televised speech, Reagan called on Americans to support increases in military spending. In the speech, excerpted below, Reagan explains the strategy of peace through nuclear deterrence, warns that the Soviet Union may be outpacing the United States in the arms race, and introduces his idea for the Strategic Defense Initiative, later described in more detail as a space-based weapons platform that would shoot down incoming missiles.

The defense policy of the United States is based on a simple premise: The United States does not start fights. We will never be an aggressor.

We maintain our strength in order to deter and defend against aggression—to preserve freedom and peace.

Since the dawn of the atomic age, we've sought to reduce the risk of war by maintaining a strong deterrent and by seeking genuine arms control. "Deterrence" means simply this: making sure any adversary who thinks about attacking the United States, or our allies, or our vital interests, concludes that the risks to him outweigh any potential gains. Once he understands that, he won't attack. We maintain the peace through our strength; weakness only invites aggression. . . .

We can't afford to believe that we will never be threatened. There have been two world wars in my lifetime. We didn't start them and, indeed, did everything we could to avoid being drawn into them. But we were ill-prepared for both. Had we been better prepared, peace might have been preserved.

For 20 years the Soviet Union has been accumulating enormous military might. They didn't stop when their forces exceeded all requirements of a legitimate defensive capability. And they haven't stopped now. During the past decade and a half, the Soviets have built up a massive arsenal of new strategic nuclear weapons—weapons that can strike directly at the United States.

As an example, the United States introduced its last new intercontinental ballistic missile, the Minute Man III, in 1969, and we're now dismantling our even older Titan missiles. But what has the Soviet Union done in these intervening years? Well, since 1969 the Soviet Union has built five new classes of ICBM's [intercontinental ballistic missiles], and upgraded these eight times. As a result, their missiles are much more powerful and accurate than they were several years ago, and they continue to develop more, while ours are increasingly obsolete. . . .

Another example of what's happened: in 1978 the Soviets had 600 intermediate range nuclear missiles based on land and were beginning to add the SS-20—a new, highly accurate, mobile missile with 3 warheads. We had none. Since then the Soviets have strengthened their lead. By the end of 1979, when Soviet leader Brezhnev declared "a balance now exists," the Soviets had over 800 warheads. We still had none. A year ago this month, Mr. Brezhnev pledged a moratorium, or freeze, on SS-20 deployment. But by last August, their 800 warheads had become more than 1,200. We still had none. Some freeze. At this time Soviet Defense Minister Ustinov announced "approximate parity of forces continues to exist." But the Soviets are still adding an average of 3 new warheads a week, and now have 1,300. These warheads can reach their targets in a matter of a few minutes. We still have none. So far, it seems that the Soviet definition of parity is a box score of 1,300 to nothing, in their favor.

So, together with our NATO allies, we decided in 1979 to deploy new weapons, beginning this year, as a deterrent to their SS-20s and as an incentive to the Soviet Union to meet us in serious arms control negotiations. We will begin that deployment late this year. At the same time, however, we're willing to cancel our program if the Soviets will dismantle theirs. This is what we've called a zero-zero plan. The Soviets are now at the negotiating table—and I think it's fair to say that without our planned deployments, they wouldn't be there.

Now let's consider conventional forces. Since 1974 the United States has produced 3,050 tactical combat aircraft. By contrast, the Soviet Union has produced twice as many. When we look at attack submarines, the United States has produced 27 while the Soviet Union has produced 61. For armored vehicles, including tanks, we have produced 11,200. The Soviet Union has produced 54,000—nearly 5 to 1 in their favor. Finally, with artillery, we've produced 950 artillery and rocket launchers while the Soviets have produced more than 13,000—a staggering 14-to-1 ratio. . . .

The final fact is that the Soviet Union is acquiring what can only be considered an offensive military force. They have continued to build far more intercontinental ballistic missiles than they could possibly need simply to deter an attack. Their conventional forces are trained and equipped not so much to defend against an attack as they are to permit sudden, surprise offensives of their own.

When I took office in January 1981, I was appalled by what I found: American planes that couldn't fly and American ships that couldn't sail for lack of spare parts and trained personnel and insufficient fuel and ammunition for essential training. The inevitable result of all this was poor morale in our Armed Forces, difficulty in recruiting the brightest young Americans to wear the uniform, and difficulty in convincing our most experienced military personnel to stay on.

There was a real question then about how well we could meet a crisis. And it was obvious that we had to begin a major modernization program to ensure we could deter aggression and preserve the peace in the years ahead. . . .

We haven't built a new long-range bomber for 21 years. Now we're building the B-1. We hadn't launched one new strategic submarine for 17 years. Now we're building one Trident submarine a year. Our land-based missiles are increasingly threatened by the many huge, new Soviet ICBM's. We're determining how to solve that problem. At the same time, we're working in the START and INF negotiations with the goal of achieving deep reductions in the strategic and intermediate nuclear arsenals of both sides.

We have also begun the long-needed modernization of our conventional forces. The Army is getting its first new tank in 20 years. The Air Force is modernizing. We're rebuilding our Navy, which shrank from about a thousand ships in the late 1960's to 453 during the 1970's. Our nation needs a superior navy to support our military forces and vital interests overseas. We're now on the road to achieving a 600-ship navy and increasing the amphibious capabilities of our marines, who are now serving the cause of peace in Lebanon. And we're building a real capability to assist our friends in the vitally important Indian Ocean and Persian Gulf region.

This adds up to a major effort, and it isn't cheap. It comes at a time when there are many other pressures on our budget and when the American people have already had to make major sacrifices during the recession. But we must not be misled by those who would make defense once again the scapegoat of the Federal budget. . . .

If the Soviet Union will join with us in our effort to achieve major arms reduction we will have succeeded in stabilizing the nuclear balance. Nevertheless, it will still be necessary to rely on the specter of retaliation, on mutual threat. And that's a sad commentary on the human condition. Wouldn't it be better to save lives than to avenge them? Are we not capable of demonstrating our peaceful intentions by applying all our abilities and our ingenuity to achieving a truly lasting stability? I think we are. Indeed, we must.

After careful consultation with my advisers, including the Joint Chiefs of Staff, I believe there is a way. Let me share with you a vision of the future which offers hope. It is that we embark on a program to counter the awesome Soviet missile threat with measures that are defensive. Let us turn to the very strengths in technology that spawned our great industrial base and that have given us the quality of life we enjoy today.

What if free people could live secure in the knowledge that their security did not rest upon the threat of instant U.S. retaliation to deter a Soviet attack, that we could intercept and destroy strategic ballistic missiles before they reached our own soil or that of our allies?

I know this is a formidable, technical task, one that may not be accomplished before the end of this century. Yet, current technology has attained a level of sophistication where it's reasonable for us to begin this effort. It will take years, probably decades of effort on many fronts.

There will be failures and setbacks, just as there will be successes and breakthroughs. And as we proceed, we must remain constant in preserving the nuclear deterrent and maintaining a solid capability for flexible response. But isn't it worth every investment necessary to free the world from the threat of nuclear war? We know it is. . . .

Tonight, consistent with our obligations of the [antiballistic missile] ABM treaty and recognizing the need for closer consultation with our allies, I'm taking an important first step. I am directing a comprehensive and intensive effort to define a long-term research and development program to begin to achieve our ultimate goal of eliminating the threat posed by strategic nuclear missiles. This could pave the way for arms control measures to eliminate the weapons themselves. We seek neither military superiority nor political advantage. Our only purpose—one all people share—is to search for ways to reduce the danger of nuclear war.

My fellow Americans, tonight we're launching an effort which holds the promise of changing the course of human history. There will be risks, and results take time. But I believe we can do it. As we cross this threshold, I ask for your prayers and your support.

Ronald Reagan, "Peace and National Security," March 23, 1983.

Document 6: The Soviets' Position on Arms Control and SDI

On November 19, 1985, Mikhail Gorbachev and Ronald Reagan met for the first time at an arms control summit in Geneva, Switzerland. On November 27, in a speech to the Soviet government, Gorbachev summarized the results of the meeting. In the portions of that address excerpted here, Gorbachev describes the United States as militant, committed to the arms race, and unwilling to listen to reason in regards to the Strategic Defense Initiative. The Soviet Union, he maintains, is committed to furthering arms control negotiations and especially to banning space-based weapons.

First of all I must say that the road to the Geneva dialogue was long and arduous for many reasons. The U.S. Administration, which came to office in the early 1980s, openly assumed a course of confrontation while rejecting the very possibility of a positive development of Soviet-American relations. I think everyone remembers even today the pitch of anti-Soviet rhetoric of those years and the character of the actions "from strength" practiced by the U.S. ruling circles.

The mutual efforts over many years to achieve the essential minimum of trust in those relations were committed to oblivion, and virtually every thread of bilateral cooperation was snapped. Detente itself was branded as being contrary to the interests of the United States of America.

Having assumed a course for reaching military superiority over the U.S.S.R., the administration went ahead with programs for nuclear and other rearmament of the U.S.A. U.S. first-strike missiles began to be deployed in Western Europe. In this way a situation was taking shape that was fraught with high-level military and political uncertainties and concomitant risks.

Lastly, there appeared a "Star Wars" program, the so-called "Strategic Defense Initiative." They in Washington became obsessed with it without giving much thought to those grave consequences which were bound to ensure if this idea were translated into practice. The plan to introduce weapons in outer space is extremely dangerous to all the peoples of the world, to all without exception.

But we also knew another thing: Such U.S. policies would inevitably clash with reality. And it happened. The Soviet Union together with its allies unequivocally declared that they would not allow military superiority over themselves. . . .

While giving a firm rebuff to the U.S. line of disrupting military-strategic equilibrium, the Soviet Union advanced large-scale peace initiatives and displayed restraint and constructiveness in the approach to the key issues of peace and security. . . .

We have put forward concrete and radical proposals in the Geneva negotiations on nuclear and space arms. What is their substance?

We have first of all proposed prohibiting space strike arms completely. We did so because the beginning of an arms race in outer space, and even only the deployment in near-Earth space of antimissile systems will not contribute to the security of any state. Hidden behind a space "shield," offensive nuclear systems will become even more dangerous.

The appearance of space strike arms could turn the present strategic balance into a strategic chaos, could cause the arms race to proceed feverishly in all directions, and could undercut one of the fundamental pillars of its limitation—the ABM Treaty. As a result, mistrust in relations between states will grow and security will diminish considerably.

Further, in the conditions of the complete prohibition of space strike weapons we have proposed halving all nuclear systems of the U.S.S.R. and the U.S. capable of reaching each other's territory and limiting the total number of nuclear warheads on such systems belonging to either side by a ceiling of 6,000. These are radical reductions of thousands of nuclear warheads. . . .

But the main thing is that the United States' stand does not envisage a ban on the creation of space strike arms. Quite the contrary, it seeks to legalize their creation. The stand assumed by the U.S. side in the question of "Star Wars" is the main obstacle to agreement on arms control. And this is not only our opinion. The governments of France, Denmark, Norway, Greece, the Netherlands, Canada and Australia refused to take part in the so-called "Strategic Defense Initiative." On the eve of the Geneva meeting the United Nations General Assembly adopted a resolution urging the leaders of the U.S.S.R. and the U.S.A. to work out effective agreements aimed at the prevention of an arms race in space and its termination on Earth. It is only the United States and some of its allies that deemed it possible not to support this clear call of the world community. A fact, as it is said, that needs no comment. . . .

The American side stubbornly insisted at the meeting on going ahead with the SDI program. We were told that the point was the development of purely defensive systems, which were not even weapons as such. We were also told that those systems would help to stabilize the situation and to get rid of nuclear weapons altogether. There was even the proposal that in some "foreseeable" future these systems would be "shared" with us and that the two sides should open the doors of their laboratories to each other.

We frankly told the President that we did not agree to these evaluations. We had thoroughly analyzed all those questions and our conclusion was unequivocal. Space weapons are not at all defensive. They can breed the dangerous illusion that it is possible to deliver a first nuclear strike from behind a space "shield" and to avert, or at least weaken, retaliation. And what are the guarantees that space weapons in themselves would not be used against targets on Earth? There is every indication that the U.S. space-based ABM system is being conceived precisely as a component of an integrated offensive complex rather than as a "shield."

Naturally, we cannot agree to the allegation that the programmed space systems are not weapons altogether. Neither can we rely on the assurances that the United States will share with us what they will develop in that field. . . .

I think that in order to achieve a real turn in our relations, which would meet the interests of the U.S.S.R., the United States and the interests of the peoples of the world, what is required are new approaches, a fresh look at many things and, what is most important, political will on the part of the leadership of the two countries. The U.S.S.R.—and I emphasized that in Geneva—does not feel enmity toward the United States, and it respects the American people. We are not building our policy on the desire to infringe on the national interests of the United States. I will say more: We would not like, for instance, a change of the strategic balance in our favor. We would not like that because such a situation will enhance the suspicion of the other side, will enhance the instability of the overall situation.

Mikhail Gorbachev, "The Geneva Meeting," *Vital Speeches of the Day*, January 15, 1986.

Document 7: Reagan's Speech Before the Brandenburg Gate

By 1987, relations between the United States and the Soviet Union had improved considerably. Reagan and Gorbachev had already met at two summit meetings, and Western observers were optimistic about the reforms taking place within the Soviet Unions. In a speech before the Brandenburg Gate at the Berlin Wall, which served as a symbolic divide between Eastern and Western Europe, Reagan acknowledged these reforms but somewhat provocatively called on Gorbachev to do more and to "tear down this wall!" The famous line was quoted often when the wall fell two years later.

In the 1950s, [Soviet leader Nikita] Khrushchev predicted: "We will bury you." But in the West today, we see a free world that has achieved a level of prosperity and well-being unprecedented in all human history. In the Communist world, we see failure, technological backwardness, declining standards of health, even want of the most basic kind— too little food. Even today, the Soviet Union still cannot feed itself. After these four decades, then, there stands before the entire world one great and inescapable conclusion: Freedom leads to prosperity. Freedom replaces the ancient hatreds among the nations with comity and peace. Freedom is the victor.

And now the Soviets themselves may, in a limited way, be coming to understand the importance of freedom. We hear much from Moscow about a new policy of reform and openness. Some political prisoners have been released. Certain foreign news broadcasts are no longer being jammed. Some economic enterprises have been permitted to operate with greater freedom from state control.

Are these the beginnings of profound changes in the Soviet state? Or are they token gestures, intended to raise false hopes in the West, or to strengthen the Soviet system without changing it? We welcome change and openness; for we believe that freedom and security go together, that the advance of human liberty can only strengthen the cause of world peace. There is one sign the Soviets can make that would be unmistakable, that would advance dramatically the cause of freedom and peace.

General Secretary Gorbachev, if you seek peace, if you seek prosperity for the Soviet Union and Eastern Europe, if you seek liberalization: Come here to this gate! Mr. Gorbachev, open this gate! Mr. Gorbachev, tear down this wall!

Ronald Reagan, "Remarks at the Brandenburg Gate," June 12, 1987.

Document 8: Reagan's and Gorbachev's Remarks After the Signing of the INF Treaty

Below are excerpts from President Reagan's and General Secretary of the Communist Party of the Soviet Union Mikhail Gorbachev's remarks at the White House on December 8, 1987, just after the signing of the Intermediate-Range Nuclear Forces (INF) Treaty.

The President. This ceremony and the treaty we're signing today are both excellent examples of the rewards of patience. It was over six years ago, November 18, 1981, that I first proposed what would come to be called the zero option. It was a simple proposal—one might say, disarmingly simple. [*Laughter*] Unlike treaties in the past, it didn't simply codify the status quo or a new arms buildup; it didn't simply talk of controlling an arms race. For the first time in history, the language of "arms control" was replaced by "arms reduction"—in this case, the complete elimination of an entire class of U.S. and Soviet nuclear missiles. . . .

The numbers alone demonstrate the value of this agreement. On the Soviet side, over 1,500 deployed warheads will be removed, and all ground-launched intermediate-range missiles, including the SS-20s, will be destroyed. On our side, our entire complement of Pershing II and ground-launched cruise missiles, with some 400 deployed warheads, will all be destroyed. Additional backup missiles on both sides will also be destroyed.

But the importance of this treaty transcends numbers. We have listened to the wisdom in an old Russian maxim. And I'm sure you're familiar with it, Mr. General Secretary, though my pronunciation may give you difficulty. The maxim is: *Dovorey no provorey*—trust, but verify.

The General Secretary. You repeat that at every meeting. [*Laughter*]

The President. I like it. [*Laughter*]

This agreement contains the most stringent verification regime in history, including provisions for inspection teams actually residing in each other's territory and several other forms of on-site inspection, as well. This treaty protects the interests of America's friends and allies. It also embodies another important principle: the need for *glasnost*, a greater openness in military programs and forces.

We can only hope that this history-making agreement will not be an end in itself but the beginning of a working relationship that will enable us to tackle the other urgent issues before us: strategic offensive nuclear weapons, the balance of conventional forces in Europe, the destructive and tragic regional conflicts that beset so many parts of our globe, and respect for the human and natural rights God has granted to all men. . . .

The General Secretary. Mr. President, ladies and gentlemen, comrades:

Succeeding generations will hand down their verdict on the importance of the event which we are about to witness. But I will venture to say that what we are going to do, the signing of the first-ever agreement eliminating nuclear weapons, has a universal significance for mankind, both from the standpoint of world politics and from the standpoint of humanism.

For everyone, and above all, for our two great powers, the treaty whose text is on this table offers a big chance at last to get onto the road leading away from the threat of catastrophe. It is our duty to take full advantage of that chance and move together toward a nuclear-free world, which holds out for our children and grandchildren and for their children and grandchildren the promise of a fulfilling and happy life without fear and without a senseless waste of resources on weapons of destruction.

We can be proud of planting this sapling, which may one day grow into a mighty tree of peace. But it is probably still too early to bestow laurels upon each other. As the great American poet and philosopher Ralph Waldo Emerson said: "The reward of a thing well done is to have done it."

So, let us reward ourselves by getting down to business. We have covered a seven-year-long road, replete with intense work and debate. One last step toward this table, and the treaty will be signed.

May December 8, 1987, become a date that will be inscribed in the history books, a date that will mark the watershed separating the era of a mounting risk of nuclear war from the era of a demilitarization of human life.

Ronald Reagan and Mikhail Gorbachev, "Remarks on Signing the INF Treaty," December 8, 1987, quoted in Ronald Reagan, ed., *Speaking My Mind: Selected Speeches.* New York: Simon & Schuster, 1989.

Document 9: Reagan Accepts Responsibility for Iran-Contra

Following the first reports of the Iran-contra scandal in November 1986, Reagan initially denied that his administration had sold arms to Iranian terrorists. However, following the release of the Tower Commission report by Congress, which found that officials in the White House had traded arms for hostages and illegally provided aid to the Nicaraguan contras, Reagan made the following remarks in a nationally televised address.

My fellow Americans:

I've spoken to you from this historic office on many occasions and about many things. The power of the presidency is often thought to reside within this Oval Office. Yet it doesn't rest here; it rests in you, the American people, and in your trust. Your trust is what gives a president his powers of leadership and his personal strength, and it's what I want to talk to you about this evening.

For the past three months, I've been silent on the revelations about Iran. And you must have been thinking: "Well, why doesn't he tell us what is happening? Why doesn't he just speak to us as he has in the past when we've faced troubles or tragedies?" Others of you, I guess, were thinking: "What's he doing hiding out in the White House?" Well, the reason I haven't spoken to you before now is this: You deserve the truth. And as frustrating as the waiting has been, I felt it was improper to come to you with sketchy reports, or possibly even erroneous statements, which would then have to be corrected, creating even more doubt and confusion. There's been enough of that.

I've paid a price for my silence in terms of your trust and confidence. But I've had to wait, as you have, for the complete story. . . .

First, let me say I take full responsibility for my own actions and for those of my administration. As angry as I may be about activities undertaken without my knowledge, I am still accountable for those activities. As disappointed as I may be in some who served me, I'm still the one who must answer to the American people for this behavior. And as personally distasteful as I find secret bank accounts and diverted funds—well, as the Navy would say, this happened on my watch.

Let's start with the part that is the most controversial. A few months ago I told the American people I did not trade arms for hostages. My heart and my best intentions still tell me that's true, but the facts and the evidence tell me it is not. As the Tower Board reported, what began as a strategic opening to Iran deteriorated, in its implementation, into trading arms for hostages. This runs counter to my own beliefs, to administration policy, and to the original strategy we had in mind. There are reasons why it happened, but no excuses. It was a mistake.

I undertook the original Iran initiative in order to develop relations with those who might assume leadership in a post-Khomeini government. It's clear from the Board's report, however, that I let my personal concern for the hostages spill over into the geopolitical strategy of reaching out to Iran. I asked so many questions about the hostages' welfare that I didn't ask enough about the specifics of the total Iran plan. . . .

Now, another major aspect of the Board's findings regards the transfer of funds to the Nicaraguan contras. The Tower Board wasn't able to find out what happened to this money, so the facts here will be left to the continuing investigations of the court-appointed Independent Counsel and the two congressional investigating committees. I'm confident the truth will come out about this matter, as well. As I told the Tower Board, I didn't know about any diversion of funds to the contras. But as president, I cannot escape responsibility. . . .

Now, what should happen when you make a mistake is this: You take your knocks, you learn your lessons, and then you move on. That's the healthiest way to deal with a problem. This in no way diminishes the importance of the other continuing investigations, but the business of our country and our people must proceed. I've gotten this message from Republicans and Democrats in Congress, from allies around the world, and—if we're reading the signals right—even from the Soviets. And of course, I've heard the message from you, the American people.

You know, by the time you reach my age, you've made plenty of mistakes. And if you've lived your life properly—so, you learn. You put things in perspective. You pull your energies together. You change. You go forward.

My fellow Americans, I have a great deal that I want to accomplish with you and for you over the next two years. And the Lord willing, that's exactly what I intend to do.

Good night, and God bless you.

Ronald Reagan, "Address to the Nation on the Tower Commission Report," March 4, 1987.

Document 10: Iran-Contra: The Final Report

In 1987, after the first preliminary reports of the Iran-contra scandal surfaced, an independent counsel was appointed to investigate any wrongdoing that may have occurred in the Reagan White House. In January 1994, after seven years of investigation, the attorney appointed to head the inquiry, Lawrence E. Walsh, released his three-volume final report. In the excerpt below, Walsh summarizes his conclusions regarding Reagan's role in the scandal.

The investigations and prosecutions have shown that high-ranking Administration officials violated laws and executive orders in the Iran/

contra matter.

Independent Counsel concluded that:

—the sales of arms to Iran contravened United States Government policy and may have violated the Arms Export Control Act;

—the provision and coordination of support to the contras violated the Boland Amendment ban on aid to military activities in Nicaragua;

—the policies behind both the Iran and contra operations were fully reviewed and developed at the highest levels of the Reagan Administration;

—although there was little evidence of National Security Council level knowledge of most of the actual contra-support operations, there was no evidence that any NSC member dissented from the underlying policy—keeping the contras alive despite congressional limitations on contra support;

—the Iran operations were carried out with the knowledge of, among others, President Ronald Reagan, Vice President George Bush, Secretary of State George P. Shultz, Secretary of Defense Caspar W. Weinberger, Director of Central Intelligence William J. Casey, and national security advisers Robert C. McFarlane and John M. Poindexter; of these officials, only Weinberger and Shultz dissented from the policy decision, and Weinberger eventually acquiesced by ordering the Department of Defense to provide the necessary arms;

—large volumes of highly relevant, contemporaneously created documents were systematically and willfully withheld from investigators by several Reagan Administration officials;

—following the revelation of these operations in October and November 1986, Reagan Administration officials deliberately deceived the Congress and the public about the level and extent of official knowledge of and support for these operations.

In addition, Independent Counsel concluded that the off-the-books nature of the Iran and contra operations gave line-level personnel the opportunity to commit money crimes. . . .

As the White House section of this report describes in detail, the investigation found no credible evidence that President Reagan violated any criminal statute. The OIC could not prove that Reagan authorized or was aware of the diversion or that he had knowledge of the extent of North's control of the contra-resupply network. Nevertheless, he set the stage for the illegal activities of others by encouraging and, in general terms, ordering support of the contras during the October 1984 to October 1986 period when funds for the contras were cut off by the

Boland Amendment, and in authorizing the sale of arms to Iran, in contravention of the U.S. embargo on such sales. The President's disregard for civil laws enacted to limit presidential actions abroad—specifically the Boland Amendment, the Arms Export Control Act and congressional-notification requirements in covert-action laws—created a climate in which some of the Government officers assigned to implement his policies felt emboldened to circumvent such laws.

President Reagan's directive to McFarlane to keep the contras alive "body and soul" during the Boland cut-off period was viewed by North, who was charged by McFarlane to carry out the directive, as an invitation to break the law. Similarly, President Reagan's decision in 1985 to authorize the sale of arms to Iran from Israeli stocks, despite warnings by Weinberger and Shultz that such transfers might violate the law, opened the way for Poindexter's subsequent decision to authorize the diversion. Poindexter told Congress that while he made the decision on his own and did not tell the President, he believed the President would have approved. North testified that he believed the President authorized it.

Lawrence E. Walsh, *Iran-Contra: The Final Report*. New York: Random House, 1994.

CHRONOLOGY

FEBRUARY 6, 1911
Ronald Wilson Reagan is born in Tampico, Illinois.

JUNE 1932
Reagan graduates from Eureka College.

1933
Reagan becomes a sports announcer for radio station WOC in Davenport, Iowa, which later merges with WHO in Des Moines.

1937
Reagan takes a screen test at Warner Brothers film studio and is offered a seven-year contract. He relocates to Hollywood and stars in his first film, *Love Is on the Air*.

JANUARY 26, 1940
Reagan marries actress Jane Wyman.

1941
Reagan stars in his two most acclaimed films, *Knute Rockne—All American* and *Santa Fe Trail*.

APRIL 1942
Reagan is drafted for World War II and serves in the Army Air Corps film unit for the next three years.

OCTOBER 23, 1947
Reagan testifies as a "friendly witness" before the House Un-American Activities Committee.

1949
Reagan and Wyman divorce.

MARCH 5, 1952
Reagan marries actress Nancy Davis.

1954
Reagan takes a job as host of the television show *General Electric Theater.* For the next eight years he serves as corporate "ambassador of goodwill" for GE, making speeches for the company around the country.

1966
Reagan is elected governor of California.

1968
Reagan seeks the Republican Party's nomination for president but loses to Richard Nixon.

1970
Reagan is elected to second term as governor of California.

1972
Reagan again seeks the presidential nomination, and again loses to Nixon.

1974
Following the Watergate scandal, Richard Nixon resigns, and Gerald Ford takes over as president.

1976
In a close race, Reagan loses the Republican presidential nomination to Gerald Ford. Ford is defeated in the presidential election, however, to Democrat Jimmy Carter.

NOVEMBER 1979
Sixty-six Americans are taken hostage by militant Islamic students in Iran.

DECEMBER 1979
The Soviet Union invades Afghanistan.

APRIL 24, 1980
Eight Americans die in a failed attempt to rescue the hostages being held in Tehran, Iran.

NOVEMBER 4, 1980
Ronald Reagan is elected president.

JANUARY 20, 1981
American hostages being held in Iran are released minutes after Reagan is sworn in as president.

FEBRUARY 18, 1981
Reagan calls for reduced taxes and domestic spending and increased defense spending.

MARCH 30, 1981
John W. Hinckley Jr. attempts to assassinate President Reagan outside the Washington Hilton Hotel. The president is shot but quickly recovers.

MAY 1, 1981
Antiwar demonstrators in Washington protest the president's policy on Central America and his proposed cuts in social spending.

AUGUST 13, 1981
Reagan signs a major tax cut, the Economic Recovery Tax Act, into law.

OCTOBER 2, 1981
As part of a military buildup, Reagan announces plans to build the B-1 bomber and the MX missile.

JUNE 12, 1982
A massive nuclear freeze demonstration takes place in New York City.

DECEMBER 2, 1982
Congress refuses to fund the MX missile.

MARCH 8, 1983
In a famous speech, Reagan denounces the nuclear freeze movement and calls the Soviet Union an "evil empire."

MARCH 23, 1983

In a nationally televised address, Reagan announces plans to build the Strategic Defense Initiative weapons system.

MAY 25, 1983

Congress agrees to fund the MX missile.

SEPTEMBER 1, 1983

U.S.-Soviet relations hit a new low after the Soviet Union shoots down Korean airliner KAL 007, with a U.S. congressman and sixty other Americans on board.

OCTOBER 23, 1983

A terrorist truck bomb explodes at U.S. Marine headquarters in Beirut, Lebanon, killing over 225 Americans.

OCTOBER 24, 1983

U.S. military forces invade Grenada, on the grounds that the new airport being constructed there was intended for Soviet military use.

DECEMBER 8, 1983

U.S.-Soviet arms control talks in Geneva, Switzerland, end with little accomplished and no date set for future negotiations.

JUNE 25, 1984

U.S. Senate passes a resolution, the Boland Amendment, cutting off all aid to the Nicaraguan contras.

NOVEMBER 6, 1984

Reagan and his vice president, George Bush, are reelected in a landslide victory over Walter Mondale and Geraldine Ferraro.

MARCH 11, 1985

Mikhail Gorbachev becomes leader of the Soviet Union.

MAY 5, 1985

Reagan's public approval ratings nosedive after a controversial visit to Bitburg Cemetery where he claims that the SS soldiers buried there were just as much victims of World War II as the Jews who were murdered in the Holocaust.

NOVEMBER 19, 1985
Reagan and Gorbachev meet for the first time in Geneva, Switzerland, and plan for more meetings in the future.

JANUARY 28, 1986
The space shuttle *Challenger* explodes after takeoff, killing all seven crew members.

FEBRUARY 1986
Mikhail Gorbachev calls for radical reform of the Soviet economy and speaks out against abuses of power within the Communist Party.

APRIL 26, 1986
An explosion occurs at the nuclear power plant in the Ukraine city of Chernobyl.

SEPTEMBER 14, 1986
President and Nancy Reagan, in joint news conference, announce a national crusade against drugs.

OCTOBER 11, 1986
Reagan and Gorbachev meet at summit in Reykjavik, Iceland, but reach no agreements.

NOVEMBER 6, 1986
The first reports of the Iran-contra affair begin to surface.

NOVEMBER 26, 1986
The Tower Commission is appointed to investigate the Iran-contra affair.

DECEMBER 6, 1986
Reagan admits he "made a mistake" in the decision to sell arms to Iran.

FEBRUARY 26, 1987
The Tower Commission holds Reagan responsible for Iran-contra, but does not accuse him of any crimes.

MARCH 4, 1987
In a public address, Reagan accepts responsibility for the Iran-contra affair.

MAY 5, 1987
Iran-contra hearings begin.

MAY 31, 1987
President Reagan calls for widespread testing in his first speech on AIDS.

JULY 7–15, 1987
Iran-contra hearings reach their climax with the televised testimony of Lieutenant Colonel Oliver North, who claims he was acting under the orders of his supervisors.

NOVEMBER 18, 1987
Congressional investigators conclude that Reagan was responsible for the Iran-contra affair.

DECEMBER 8, 1987
At a summit in Washington, D.C., Reagan and Gorbachev sign the intermediate-range nuclear forces (INF) treaty, the first in which the two superpowers commit to dismantling an entire class of nuclear missiles.

MAY 29–JUNE 2, 1988
Reagan visits Moscow for the fourth summit meeting between the two nations.

NOVEMBER 8, 1988
George Bush wins presidential election over Michael Dukakis.

JANUARY 11, 1989
President Reagan delivers his farewell address.

MAY 4, 1989
Lieutenant Colonel Oliver North convicted on charges stemming from Iran-contra affair, but the conviction is later overturned.

JUNE 5, 1989
The first democratic election in Poland in forty years brings an end to Communist rule in that country.

JULY 1989
Gorbachev announces that Eastern European countries are free to decide their own political futures.

NOVEMBER 9, 1989
East Germany opens its borders with West Germany, and celebrators begin tearing down the Berlin Wall. Between October 1989 and January 1990, the Communist governments of Czechoslovakia, Hungary, East Germany, Romania, and Bulgaria are all toppled.

JULY 1, 1991
The Warsaw Pact formally comes to an end.

AUGUST 19–29, 1991
After a failed coup attempt against Mikhail Gorbachev, Boris Yeltsin comes to power and the Communist Party is disbanded.

DECEMBER 25, 1991
Gorbachev resigns as president of the Soviet Union. The following day, the union formally dissolves.

JANUARY 1994
Independent counsel Lawrence Walsh releases his final report on the Iran-contra affair. Without accusing Reagan of any crime, it is nevertheless the most critical of the three reports on Iran-contra.

NOVEMBER 5, 1994
Reagan announces that he has Alzheimer's disease.

FOR FURTHER RESEARCH

HERBERT L. ABRAMS, 'The President Has Been Shot': Confusion, Disability, and the 25th Amendment. Stanford, CA: Stanford University Press, 1994.

MARTIN ANDERSON, Revolution: The Reagan Legacy. Stanford, CA: Hoover Institution Press, 1988.

WESLEY M. BAGBY, America's International Relations Since World War I. New York: Oxford University Press, 1999.

ADRIANA BOSCH, Reagan: An American Story. New York: TV Books, 1998.

ROBERT BUSBY, Reagan and the Iran-Contra Affair: The Politics of Presidential Recovery. New York: St. Martin's Press, 1999.

LOU CANNON, President Reagan: The Role of a Lifetime. New York: Simon & Schuster, 1991.

THEODORE DRAPER, A Very Thin Line: The Iran-Contra Affairs. New York: Hill and Wang, 1991.

DINESH D'SOUZA, Ronald Reagan: How an Ordinary Man Became an Extraordinary Leader. New York: Free Press, 1997.

WILBUR EDEL, The Reagan Presidency: An Actor's Finest Performance. New York: Hippocrene Books, 1992.

JOHN LEWIS GADDIS, We Now Know: Rethinking Cold War History. New York: Oxford University Press, 1998.

DAVID W. HOUCK AND AMOS KIEWE, EDS., Actor, Ideologue, and Politician: The Public Speeches of Ronald Reagan. Westport, CT: Greenwood Press, 1993.

HAYNES JOHNSON, Sleepwalking Through History: America in the Reagan Years. New York: Anchor Books, 1992.

PETER B. LEVY, Encyclopedia of the Reagan-Bush Years. Westport, CT: Greenwood Press, 1996.

MYRON A. MARTY, Daily Life in the United States, 1960–1990: Decades of Discord. Westport, CT: Greenwood Press, 1997.

EDWIN MEESE III, *With Reagan: The Inside Story.* Washington, DC: Regnery, 1992.

DAVID MERVIN, *Ronald Reagan and the American Presidency.* New York and London: Longman, 1990.

EDMUND MORRIS, *Dutch: A Memoir of Ronald Reagan.* New York: Random House, 1999.

WILLIAM KER MUIR, *The Bully Pulpit: The Presidential Leadership of Ronald Reagan.* Washington, DC: Institute for Contemporary Studies, 1992.

DON OBERDORFER, *From the Cold War to a New Era: The United States and the Soviet Union, 1983–1991.* Baltimore: Johns Hopkins University Press, 1998.

WILLIAM E. PEMBERTON, *Exit with Honor: The Life and Presidency of Ronald Reagan.* Armonk, NY: M.E. Sharpe, 1997.

KEVIN PHILIPS, *The Politics of Rich and Poor: Wealth and the American Electorate in the Reagan Aftermath.* New York: Random House, 1990.

RONALD REAGAN, *An American Life.* New York: Simon & Schuster, 1990.

RONALD REAGAN, *Speaking My Mind: Selected Speeches.* New York: Simon & Schuster, 1989.

RONALD REAGAN, MICHAEL REAGAN, AND JAMES D. DENNEY, EDS., *The Common Sense of an Uncommon Man : The Wit, Wisdom, and Eternal Optimism of Ronald Reagan.* New York: Thomas Nelson, 1998.

MICHAEL SCHALLER, *Reckoning with Reagan: America and Its Presidency in the 1980s.* New York: Oxford University Press, 1992.

BOB SCHIEFFER AND GARY PAUL GATES, *The Acting President.* New York: E.P. Dutton, 1989.

JOSEPH SHATTAN, *Architects of Victory: Six Heroes of the Cold War.* Washington, DC: Heritage Foundation, 1999.

JOHN W. SLOAN, *The Reagan Effect: Economics and Presidential Leadership.* Lawrence: University of Kansas Press, 1999.

DEBORAH HART STROBER AND GERALD S. STROBER, *Reagan: The Man and His Presidency.* Boston: Houghton Mifflin, 1998.

LAWRENCE E. WALSH, *Firewall: The Iran-Contra Conspiracy and Cover-Up.* New York: W.W. Norton, 1997.

INDEX

democratic elections in, 143
Hasenfus captured in, 151
Reagan's policy of aid to
    anticommunists in, 76, 82, 83,
    125, 136
    illegality of, 140, 141
Nixon, Richard, 40, 42, 91, 97, 196
    and policy of détente towards
    Russia, 25
    and policy on federalism, 47
    presidency of destroyed in
    Watergate cover-up, 151
    Reagan's loss of Republican
    nomination to, 20
    resignation prompted by threat of
    impeachment,163
    respected but not well liked, 193,
    195
Noonan, Peggy, 185
North, Oliver, 136, 140, 141, 154
    background of, 144
    role in Iran-contra affair, 145–46,
    150, 155
        and attempt to conceal evidence,
        152, 160, 166
        and firing of, 159
        announced to press, 153
North American Aerospace Defense
    Command, 102

Oberdorfer, Don, 26
oil industry, 69
O'Neill, Tip, 145, 182, 188, 196
Operation Staunch, 147, 148
Organization of East Caribbean
    States, 84

Packwood, Robert, 196
Pahlavi, Mohammad Reza (shah of
    Iran), 128, 135, 146
Pemberton, William E., 15–16, 18,
    140
Peres, Shimon, 148
*Peril and Promise: A Commentary on
    America* (Chancellor), 189

Perle, Richard, 100
Peterson, Paul, 23
Philadelphia Inquirer (newspaper),
    73
Phillips, Kevin, 23–24, 73
Plante, Bill, 158
Poindexter, John, 142, 146, 155
    loyalty to Reagan, 149
    resignation of, 159
Policy Review (magazine), 83
Politics of Rich and Poor, The
    (Phillips), 24
Posner, Richard, 51
poverty, 70, 71
    see also welfare
Powell, Colin, 103
*President Reagan: The Role of a
    Lifetime* (Cannon), 155
"Program for Economic Recovery,
    A," (Reagan's message to
    Congress), 59, 63, 64
Public Papers of the Presidents, 181

Rafsanjani, Ali Akbar, 155
*Reagan Effect: Economics and
    Presidential Leadership, The*
    (Sloan), 22
Reagan, Jack (father), 15, 16
Reagan, Nancy Davis (wife), 18
Reagan, Nelle (mother), 15
Reagan, Ronald Wilson, 34
    achievements of, 46, 48, 86–88
        limitations in, 24, 47, 62, 63
    and profound influence of,
    44–45
        including spread of greed in
        society, 58
        known as Reagan Revolution,
        23
    also called "the Great
    Communicator," 32, 50
        Cold War speech of, 77–78
        emotional appeal of, 185–86
        with liking for anecdotes, 20, 59,
        182